BOULDERING
in the Canadian Rockies

Rocky
Mountain Books
Calgary–Victoria–Vancouver

BOULDERING
in the Canadian Rockies

Chris Fink
Marcus Norman
Daren Tremaine

Acknowledgements

Dan Archambault, Dave Carley, Rich Castello, Roger Chayer, Randy Coleman, Alan Derbyshire, Dale Diduck, Dave Dornian, Jack Firth, Ben Gadd, Derek Galloway, Brian Greenwood, Ian Groll, Ian Hayes, Trent Hoover, Jeff Horne, Paddy Jerome, Ryan Johnstone, Jon Jones, Louis-Julian Roy, Urs Kallen, Jessica Klassen, Zoë Kozub, Eddie Laporte, JD Leblanc, Seth Mason, Jeff Perron, Lev Pinter, John Martin, Malcolm McInnis, Paul McSorely, Tim Mooney, Dung Nguyen, Chris Perry, Chic Scott, Raphael Slawinski, Knut Rokne, Steve Stank, Bill Stark, Walson Tai, Margo Talbot, Bruno Tasson, Theresa Tremaine, Alan and Alisen Tremaine, Simon Villenuve, Kevin Wilson, Calgary Climbing Centre, Flashed Climbing—all of these people contributed to the success of this project.

We acknowledge the financial support of the Government of Canada through the Book Publishing Industry Development Program (BPIDP) and the support of the Alberta Foundation for the Arts for our publishing program.

Published by Rocky Mountain Books
108, 17665-66A Ave., Surrey, BC V3S 2A7
Printed and bound in Canada by
RMB Houghton Boston, Saskatoon

National Library of Canada Cataloguing in Publication Data

Fink, Chris, 1976-

Bouldering in the Canadian Rockies / Chris Fink, Marcus Norman, Daren Tremaine.

ISBN 1-894765-38-9

1. Rock climbing--Rocky Mountains, Canadian (B.C. and Alta.)--Guidebooks.* 2. Rocky Mountains, Canadian (B.C. and Alta.)--Guidebooks.* I. Tremaine, Daren Paul, 1969- II. Norman, Marcus, 1972- III. Title.

GV199.44.C22R62785 2003   796.52'23'09711   C2003-910627-6

CONTENTS

Introduction – 7
Grading & American History – 8
Ethics & the Rocks – 9
History of Bouldering –10
Area Map –14

Bouldering Areas

Glenwood Erratic – 14
Frank Slide – 18
Big Rock – 30
Beddington Area – 43
The White Buddha – 52
Big Choss – 66
Rundle Rock Area – 88
EEOR – 90
Grassi Lakes – 92
Jura Creek – 98
Takakkaw Falls – 102
Cathedral Forest – 107
Weeping Boulders – 121
Jasper Area – 127
Cadomin Boulders – 142

Front cover: Seth Mason on Only the Strong V10, The Love Den.
Back cover: Zoë Kozub on The Tossinator V7, The Love Den.

Big Choss. Photo: Marcus Norman

Bouldering in the Land of Perpetual Winter

It's hip, it's here. That's right folks after years of obscurity and disrespect, bouldering has gone mainstream. Sport climbing is dead. Hide your rope and draws, it's now a badge of honour to have never tied-in. This new trend is so user-friendly it makes rollerblading look like a high-commitment endeavour. Grab a pad, some chalk and booties and hop on the bandwagon.

Don't be discouraged by the fact that some of the problems in this guide were done over 50 years ago, or that bouldering has already been dropped from the X-games. Bouldering is **the** hot new sport. And what does a new/old sport need to really get rolling? How about a guidebook, complete with locations and descriptions of problems (so you don't need any creativity), and grades (so you can pump up your ego). That's right—we're here to pimp the Rockies. Why? Well I'm quite confident it's not for the money. It just seems like it's about time to get all of the right info out about what's been happening around here for the past 50 years.

Perhaps one of bouldering's biggest attractions locally is the climate. The climbing season at some of the best crags in the area is only 3-4 months long. However, sunny and 5°C pretty much describes perfect bouldering and the typical weather around Calgary for much of the year.

This book covers many areas big and small. A few fledgling rocks have been omitted but with any luck the problems at these places will be all cleaned up, sent, and ready for the next edition.

Grades

We know that there are inconsistencies in the grades given in this book. Some people will even think that these grades are dead wrong. We've tried to keep things reasonable, but the guide covers a wide geographical area, several different rock types, and is compiled from the reports of three very different authors—none of whom have done every problem. Most of the problems described in this book were established with the spirit of "Hey that looks good, lets climb it", rather than getting all over focused on grades. Climbing that way is kind of fun. So please don't take the grades in this edition of the guide as gospel, and we'll do our best to clean things up in the next edition. A big part of gaining consensus is feedback from **you**, the reader.

Warning

There is a popular misconception that bouldering is somehow safer than roped climbing. Although the average boulder problem is much shorter than a roped route, every fall is a ground fall. On many boulder problems, a single fall from the wrong spot could easily end in a trip to the hospital or worse. Many experienced climbers have had their most serious injuries while bouldering. Try not to boulder alone. The best safety solution is a realistic concept of your ability, a good crash pad, an attentive spotter, and a constant awareness of where you're going to land when you fall. And, uh ... the cushions off your mom's old couch? They don't qualify as a good crash pad. Your ankles are definitely worth shelling out a little cash for a good pad. Check out the various books and articles out there for spotting techniques and such.

Grading & American History

The legendary John Gill created one of the first boulder problem grading schemes. His system is a sliding scale designed to let boulderers know how they stand versus the rest of the boulderers of their generation. This keeps things interesting because every couple of years as climbing standards rise, the grading scale must also rise. The B-scale has only three ratings:

B1 Equivalent to the hardest moves that have been done on roped routes.

B2 Harder than B1

B3 An incredibly hard boulder problem that has yet to be repeated. As soon as a B3 problem is repeated it is downgraded to B2.

In 1969 Gill defined B1 as 5.10. Using Gill's definitions and today's standards, B1 is equivalent to the crux moves on hard 5.14. A problem such as Dream Time, which has been repeated, is only B2. The problem with the B grade system is quite obvious, most of the boulder problems in this book aren't hard enough to even register on the scale.

In this guide we've used the V-Scale which is now pretty much the standard for all of North America. Created by John Sherman, who has selflessly lent the V from his nickname Vermin. It is an open-ended grading scale that currently ranges from V0 to about V15. The V grading scale is fixed. In fact, in his guide to Hueco Tanks, Sherman even includes standards for each V grade to prevent the scale from slipping. V grades are only related to the difficulty of a short series of moves. Objective hazards such as falling off a high ball and impaling your spine on a sharp rock, are not factored into the grade. Because every person has a different body type, everyone has a different idea of grades. This observation, however, has evolved into a key element of the climber social structure. Without grading controversies most climbers would have nothing to talk about. The V scale is intended to grade hard problems. You'll probably find that V0 is a catch-all grade for everything from a sidewalk, to problems on which you may have to try.

Despite some popular misconception, there is no correlation between V grades and the modern interpretation of the Yosemite Decimal System (YDS) used at crags. Originally the YDS was supposed to grade the hardest move on a route. Currently the YDS system is used like the French system to grade the overall nature of a pitch. Factors such as length, rests, and the location of the cruxes all factor into a route grade. For example one route may have a good rest before its V4 crux and be graded 12b, another 12b route may be very sustained but have no moves harder than V2.

Author's Disclaimer

The information in this book is entirely related to imaginary areas. Any relation to real places is entirely coincidental. Efforts to relate this information to real places is done solely at your own peril.

Ethics and the Rocks

Needless to say the rocks covered in this guide are valuable natural resources, many times sustaining diverse and important ecosystems. The following is a guide to opening new problems and needs to be followed to the letter:

1) Use only nylon brushes to clean moss and debris. Wire brushes are harder than limestone and will remove all texture from the holds, destroying the problem.
2. When cleaning off a boulder top, remove all loose stone and debris.
3. Should a rock have a moss bed on top, clean the face and drop off at the lip. If this screws up your idea of a top-out—tough.
4. Do not place bolts on boulders, do not leave slings on trees.
5. Do not use chisels or other equipment to enhance holds.
6. Be sensitive to landings. If dangerous objects loom, remove them only if the overall area impact is minimal.
7. Do not build artificial landings.
8. Pack out all litter and refuse. If a call of nature occurs, use a public restroom or in the event of an emergency—do your business far from climbs and water sources.
9. Be respectful of others rights to peaceful bouldering. Loud dogs, stereos and T-shirts can be left at home.
10. Be respectful of landowners and administrators. They have the final say on access, so obey their rules.
11. Avoid damaging live trees and greenery—these things add to a location, even if they are in the way of your uberproject.
12. Avoid climbing near native pictographs—these are valuable and sensitive historical artifacts

Disclaimer

There are inherent risks in bouldering. While the authors have done their best to provide accurate information and to point out potential hazards, conditions may change owing to weather and other factors. It is up to the users of this guide to learn the necessary skills for safe bouldering and to exercise caution in potentially hazardous areas. Please read the Introduction and particularly the "Warning" on page 7,

Boulderers using this book do so entirely at their own risk and the authors and publishers disclaim any liability for injury or other damage that may be sustained by anyone using the access and/or bouldering routes described.

HISTORY OF BOULDERING

The history of bouldering in the Rockies is long in tradition, but short on coverage. The Big Rock near Okotoks, Rundle Rock, Laporte's Leap, and the Kain Hut area in the Bugaboos are the primary progenitors to today's hotspots. Since the 1950s, climbers have been all over these rocks, but unfortunately nobody bothered to take notes on what went down.

For half a century now climbers have been visiting these areas among others. Back in the day, it would be a common occurrence to run into such legends as John Laughlan, John Martin or the mighty Brian Greenwood climbing high at the Big Rock or getting funky at Rundle Rock. These guys were having fun, getting scared, and honing their moves—but with one eye directed towards bigger things. It can be said that until recently, bouldering was a means to an end, and lacked the credibility to even warrant a guide. Times and attitudes change. Fun is fun despite the setting and scurrying about the blocs got some positive exposure. Many thanks to the French, who continually supported the efforts and achievements of climbers pushing the technical limits in Fontainebleau, even when it wasn't cool.

Here in the Rockies, climbers saw the measurable impact that training, through bouldering, had on sport climbing. Many of those people realized both sports had the potential to be equally rewarding. The arrival of indoor climbing gyms complete with bouldering walls bolstered progress as well. Many of today's boulderers emerged from the gym environment, strong from endless hours of plastic-pulling.

But let's back up a bit...

In the late 60's and early 70's a British invasion of the Rockies began with the arrivals of Jack Firth, Ian Hayes, Jeff Horne, Bug's McKeith, Rob Wood, Jon Jones, Chris Perry, Gerry Rogan and George Homer. Also contributing problems at the time was visiting American Paul Sibly. These folks joined the CMC (Calgary Mountain Club) whose members were regulars at Wednesday evening beer night. Big Rock and other nearby erratics became a home-away-from-home for those with roots in the Peak district and other grit zones. Many classic problems were sent in the 60's and 70's, a testament to this generation's skill. Included is Jack Firth's ascent of the *Firth Jug Haul*—now one of the most popular problems at Big Rock. Allan Derbyshire is well known for repeating many of the classics at Big Rock, and adding a few of his own. Keep in mind all of this occurred without the soft loving comfort of a crashpad. Many of the problems done in this era are still test pieces today—both in terms of difficulty and commitment.

After the initial flurry of activity, local standards progressed slowly until the 80's and the birth of sport climbing. With the focus now on physical ability, bouldering was quickly recognized as the perfect way to improve technique and build the power required for hard sport routes. The first indication of what could be achieved when talented climbers focused entirely on technical difficulty came in 1988 when Jason Holt sent *The Resurrection* at Big Rock—despite this being a world class effort and a quantum leap in local standards this ascent went relatively unheralded. It would be 7 years before another local problem of similar difficulty would be established. During this time lots of local climbers were bouldering hard on plastic, but when it came time to go outdoors everyone would head south to areas such as Hueco. Traditional areas such as Big Rock and Rundle Rock had been written off at the time as nothing but a bunch of 5.10's and 11's—unworthy of a highly trained sport climbing hone master.

Around 1994, Rick Connover and JD LeBlanc decided that there had to be good hard local bouldering. Inspired by JD's stories of Jason's first ascent of *The Resurrection* they headed for Big Rock. The result of this foray—and many solo trips by Rick—was problems such as *Bob's Liquor Mart* and *The Torment of Evil*. Local standards had once again started to rise. Rick's 30 minute first ascent of *The Insurrection* was truly an inspired effort. Next on the scene at Big Rock was Seth Mason. Seth has made his mark in many established and developing areas, he simply shows up and does the first ascent of the hardest lines. His contributions include *Jabba*, *X-wing*, *Y-wing*, and *Mon Cal*. Kevin Wilson also deserves a nod for having done *The Full Torment of Evil* both ways.

Always curious whether his sport venue Prairie Creek had a sunny south facing aspect, Daren Tremaine decided to do a little reconnaissance on the other side of the ridge. The result was The White Buddha. It's not your typical bouldering area, but is blessed with a huge concentration of problems, and amazingly warm temperatures. Starting in 1995 Daren and Rich Castillo got things started with most of the early first ascents including *Trout Fishing in America*, *Segundo*, and *95% Man*. Once again Seth Mason showed up and set the standard with his ascent of *Right Potatoe Bonda* in 1996. About as hard as any problem in North America at the time, this problem still remains among the hardest in the province. Recently Kevin Wilson has repeated pretty much everything, put up a few lines of his own, and invented an endless series of super hard eliminates. His contributions include *Heizenberg's Uncertainty Principle* and *Dodge This*.

The scene at Big Rock in the 70s.
Photo: Courtesy of Diana Knaak.

Never satisfied with endlessly repeating the same old problems, Theresa Tremaine, Daren Tremaine and Ryan Johnstone turned their attention to the neglected and despised rubble heap at the base of Yamnuska around 1999. Appropriately christened Big Choss, these boulders have been occasionally top-roped, soloed, and dissed—but mostly been ignored, for years. In the mid-seventies, the Rocky Mountain YMCA ran courses each summer based out of teepees, which were set up near one of the many small lakes in the area. Among other activities, participants would climb and explore the boulders. The idea was to gain some sort of personal enlightenment through a connection with nature. Apparently, this concept didn't sell too well in red neck Alberta, and the camp was short lived. It took a different perspective to "mine out" the potential this place had. Landings were levelled, choss cleaned, and eventually gems began to take shape. The developers have found both convenience and quality in these rocks and have established perhaps a hundred new problems. At the same time, and operating entirely independently, Dave Kenefick was also searching the boulders for good problems.

Further north, Trent Hoover was busy at the Rock Gardens, establishing Jasper's first hard problem called *Genesis*. Dan Gable upped the ante with the ascent of *Rabbit and the Moon* at Lost Boys Crag. Hoover's independent guide Small Stones came out in 2000—the first bouldering guide of its kind in Alberta. Laporte's Leap and The Genesis Boulders near the Maligne River saw action as did the Kitchener Slide and Jura Creek. Dung Nguyen and Chris Fink have been in the mix as well. Their search for new problems in the Bow Valley and beyond have yielded numerous results.

The Frank Slide began to swing into gear thanks to contributions from Ian Groll, Evan Erickson, Lev Pinter, and Kevin Wilson. Indeed an eerie place to spend a day, knowing the tragic history.

Slide paths can be areas of easy access for the lazy boulderer. Case in point, Cathedral Forest. Although an obscure venue for many years, seeing the occasional trip by veterans like Eddie Laporte and Ben Gadd, Cathedral took the concerted efforts of several people to come into its own. Randy Coleman and Marcus Norman spent the better part of an entire summer—3 days a week—charting, exploring and climbing these rocks. Help from friends like Lev Pinter and Scott Milton, solidified and expanded the number of routes to well over a hundred in a short amount of time. Of note are Seth Mason's first ascents of *Menubrium* and *6 of 9*, both hovering in the V10 range.

All in all, the Canadian Rockies is slowly transforming itself into a destination for bouldering. New problems, areas and ideas will be explored as the independent sport of bouldering continues to grow. Today's testpieces have a direct link to past triumphs, as do today's climbers. By appreciating contributions early boulderers made to the current scene, we begin to see bouldering not as something new, not as something old, but as something worth doing.

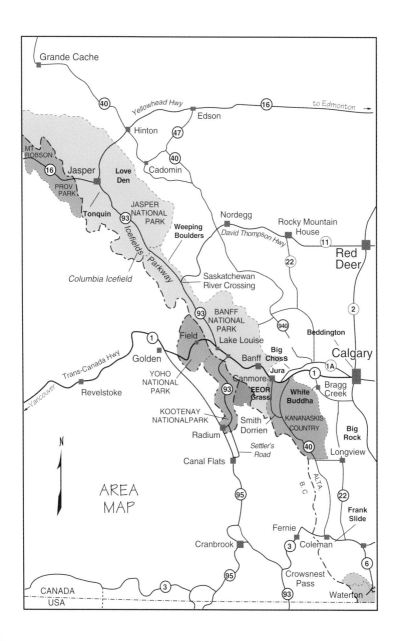

Grande Cache

Yellowhead Hwy · to Edmonton →

Edson

Hinton

MT ROBSON

Jasper · Love Den

PROV PARK

Tonquin

JASPER NATIONAL PARK

Cadomin

Icefields Parkway

Nordegg · Rocky Mountain House

Weeping Boulders

David Thompson Hwy

Columbia Icefield

Red Deer

Saskatchewan River Crossing

BANFF NATIONAL PARK

Field · Lake Louise

Big Choss

Trans-Canada Hwy

Golden · Banff · Jura

Beddington

Calgary

YOHO NATIONAL PARK

Canmore

EEOR Grassi

Bragg Creek

Vancouver

Revelstoke

White Buddha

KOOTENAY NATIONALPARK

Smith Dorrien

KANANASKIS COUNTRY

Big Rock

Radium

Settler's Road

Longview

N

Canal Flats

AREA MAP

ALTA

B.C.

Frank Slide

Fernie

Cranbrook

Coleman

Crowsnest Pass

CANADA
USA

Waterton

The Glenwood Erratic is the second largest erratic in the train and about 45 min from Lethbridge. In Stalkers report the boulder was located just outside of the town Glenwoodville which is now just called Glenwood. The boulder should be visible to the south heading east on 505 to RDG 270 or 264 from Glenwood, 0.4miles east one mile south. The problems range from V0 to about V7 and there is scope for many harder problems.

1. **Eastern Decent V0**
   Mainly just a descent
2. **Pop Goes Your Wrist** V3**
   Sds Hard sit and move left before the ledge to a jug then to top underclings and thumb catches.
3. **Years Ago*** Sds V3 Start standing V1**
4. **Josh's Problem V2**
   Start with thin hands, reaching high to a blocky looking crimp and up
5. **Bleed It Like You Mean It* Sds V7**
   Start standing V3 on small starting side pulls move to crack then reach high to a sidepull and up.
6. **Sheep That Kick Sds V4**
   Jump start V1 to the crack and straight up. Extend sds of #5 before the crack at V6.

7. **Pop Goes Your Wrist V4**
   Sds as #6 but before the big sidepull flake move right on small crimps to a jug and straight up.

8. **Reachlarge V4**
   Big stretches and is considered a tall person problem. Crux is at the top!
   Sds V4 +

9. **Unnamed Sds V3**
   Start as for #8 but move right at the good holds. Start standing at V1.

10. **Hatch s Got Bad Grammer V2**
    Thin move straight up join up with #9.

11. **Western Origins V1**
    Crux at the top!

12. **Brett s PJ V0**
    Mostly a descent.

13. **Unnamed V0**
    Start under small roof then over lip and up to the top.

14. **Unnamed V3**
    Sit start, left hand out high and right on low jug then joins the arête and move left.

15. Stigma*** V3
One hand on each side of arête and up. Once over the lip move left to a sidepull then a jug.

16. Unnamed V0
Boring start with the crux at the top. Searching required on this problem and has a textbook bad landing.

17. Stopping a Freefall V1
Crux top out so pads are highly recommended.

18. High Quality Crack Sds V2
Start on sidepull and follow flaky holds left half way up then reach for a horizontal crack and to the top.

19. Fix It With Duct Tape Sds V3/4
Start on small crimps and straight up eventually getting to a hidden jug in the crack then top out.

20. Crack Kills Sds V3, Start standing V2
2 or 3 feet right of #19 with hands on crack then high step and mantle the mini-roof to get to the same hidden jug as on #19 and top out.

21. High Flying Sds V3, Start standing V2
As for the same start as #20 but at the mantle move a bit to the right and dyno for the top.

22. Unnamed V0
Follow the Jugs diagonal right all the way up to the top.

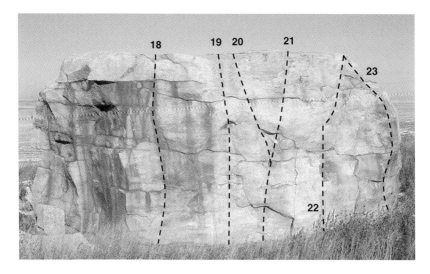

23. Eons of Polish Sds V4
Bad feet to start and go with left hand to flaky jug then right to sharp holds, high step right leg around arête and straight up.

24. Unnamed V0
Turn the lip on the small boulder beside the main boulder.

From the top of the main boulder you'll see a small boulder in the distance.

25. Buttered Traverse V1
Heel hook traverse starting on the right going left.

26. Unnamed V1
Start in the centre of the boulder and straight up to the lip. One move wonder.

FRANK SLIDE

The Frank Slide occurred in the early hours of April 29, 1903 killing 76 unsuspecting people. Approximately thirty million cubic metres of limestone fell from the east face of Turtle Mountain, spreading millions of boulders across the valley and as high as one hundred and fifty metres up the other side. The rockslide left hundreds of large boulders on the surface; mega-ultra-bouldering potential. In the last couple of years the areas has been scouted and worked on by boulderers from Edmonton, Calgary and Lethbridge: Erik Evanson, Lev Pinter, Kyle Marco, Josh Comhau, Reg Brown, Chris Humphries, Justin Lacelle, Bryne MacLachlan. Ian Groll, Seth Mason, Kevin Wilson all deserve credit for development for the development of bouldering in the area. This guide is an introduction to the bouldering here. Much work remains to be done.

Getting There
From Calgary you can either take Hwy. 22 south or Hwy. 2 south to Hwy. 3. Follow Hwy. 3 west to just before Frank where the highway passes right through the slide. About 3.5 hours from Calgary. About 1 hour from Lethbridge.

GPS
Because locating the more remote boulders on the Frank Slide is difficult, GPS coordinates have been provided. Eventually, as the area gets more developed, specific areas will be mapped so that boulders may more easily find their way around. The Datum used for the GPS readings is NAD83

Camping
There is good free camping next to the highway in Bellevue that comes highly recommended. There are tables outhouses, firewood and grills. This is a bouldering dirt bags paradise. Donations I'm sure are greatly appreciated.

Albatross boulder taken around 1911. Provincial Archives of Alberta A 1771.

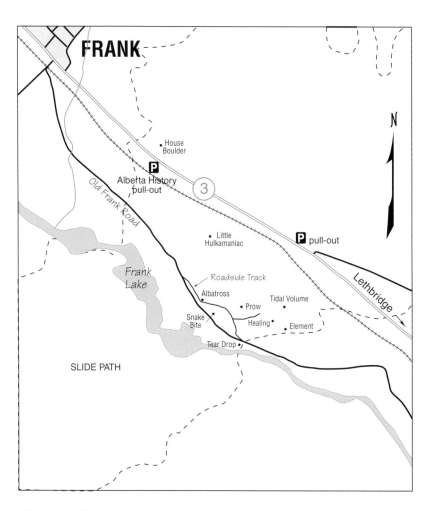

House Boulder Area

As you drive on Highway 3 through the slide heading west you will see a large boulder on the right opposite a pull-out at an Alberta History sign. Park here and cross the highway to the large house-sized boulder. There are 20+ problems by Lev Pinter & Seth Mason.

City of
Giants

House Boulder
Area

Mink Boulders

The Other
Side

Old Frank Road Boulders

Just past the slide, heading west on Highway 3, there is a turn-off on the left to the old road that was rerouted in 1906 and is now called 152 St. Cross the railroad tracks and bear left. This is the access for most of the problems recorded here. There are several pull-outs for parking along the road. Distances along the road mentioned in the descriptions following are from Hwy. 3 at Frank.

1. **Chossorama* V4**
   1.0 km along the road on the left. Heelhooks then out left to a hueco and then straight up.

2. **Lizard Head V?**
   In a small valley on the left about 100 m beyond Chossorama. Sds on the right side of the head.

Roadside Traverse Boulder
3. **Roadside Traverse* V6**
   1.5 km along road on the right. There is parking either side of the boulders. Traverse the lip from left to right.

Albatross

The large boulder a short distance up the Roadside Track.

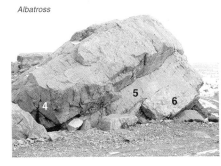

Albatross

4. **Road Runner Excavation Company V8**
   Lev Pinter's cave problem.
5. **Albatross V4**
   Sds in V-notch and work up to an undercling and a big stretch.
6. **Groove of the Move V6**
7. **Shutdown** ** V5**
   Sds on flake and out of the roof and finish out right.

Triforce Boulder

On Roadside Track just west of Albatross

Shutdown

8. **Triforce V6**
   Sds down and right and cross over to the top of the triangle.

Triforce

Snake Bite Boulder

49 35.291N 114 23.615W

Snake Bite Boulder

9. **Snake Bite V1**
10. **Brett's Ugly Face V3**
11. **Apple Shampoo V2**
12. **V2**
    Left variation of #11.

Fender Boulder

A brown-coloured boulder at the side of the road opposite a power pole with a nesting platform

13. Fender*** V6

Edge to left gaston, crossover to crimp and throw to a sloper and a scary top-out.

Fender

14. Josh's Problem V3

On the boulder right next to Fender
Sds on right on edges heading out right.

Josh's Problem

Teardrop Boulder

Teardrop Boulder

49 35.208N 114 23.528 W
By the river at 1.8 km

15. V0**

Sds on jug to undercling.

16. V3

Same start as #13 left to thin face.

17. V2

Sds as for #13 to flake and arête finish.

18. Bear Hug V2

Straight up flake and arête.

Smashing

19. Smashing V3

Close to The Prow.
Sds on undercling and lip. match and mantle.

The Prow 49 35.305N 114 23.497W

20. Small Bicep Man V2
Sds Arête.

21. V1
Sds Straightforward.

22. G is for Grunt V1
Seam.

23. Bent Backwards V4/5

24. V0
Arête.

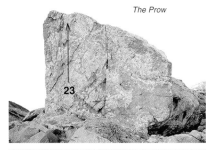
The Prow

Unnamed Boulder 49 35.259N 114 23.354W

25. V0.

26. V0

27. White Lightening V2

28. Drift Net V4
Sds in middle of the face.

29. V2/3

Drift Net

The Healing Boulder
49 35.264N 114 23.350W

30. V0
Sds face to dihedral.

31. Jahaely V3
Sds on flake out right to face and crimps.

32. V4
Sds out left friction high steps.

33. The Sage V5
Start standing on crimp to right of flake.

34. Flake Route V0

35. Origins V2/3
Sds on horizontal edges and seam then out on arête slopers

36. V2
Sds right of Healing Arête.

37. Healing Arête* V5**

38. V4.

Healing Boulder

Shock Boulder

49 35.267N 114 23.323W
A group of 3 boulders a few metres
north of healing Boulder

39. In Fetus We Trust V4

40. Shock Load V3

41. V0

42. Ballerina Kick V3
   Sds left and right variations.

Shock Boulder

Ballerina Kick

Shock Boulder #2 V0

Relentless Boulder

A short distance to the south of
Healing Boulder

43. Scarleg V1
   Left edge of face.

44. Relentless V6
   Sds V7

45. Operation Fricking Dihedral V3
   The obvious dihedral. Sds V4

46. Project

Element Boulder
49 35.261N 114 23.354W

47 The 5th Element*** V2
Pinch and turn the lip.
48. Element V2 Face left of #43.
49. Open Road V2
Arête.

Tidal Volume Boulder
49 35.289N 114 23.300W

50. V3
Scooping face.
51. Flight School 101 V3
Dyno eliminate to the lip.
52. Killer S's
V0 Left of arête.
53. Killer B's V3/4
Sds on sloper.
54. Serial Killer*** V5
Iron Cross to sloper and rail.

55. Abdominator V2
Close to Tidal Volume Boulder
Start laying down and toe hook the
lip and do an upside down sit-up to
the lip and campus.

Element Boulder

Serial Killer

Abdominator

Serial Killer

56. Nintendo 69*** V6
49 35.299N 114 23.287W
Sds under roof on rail with left and crimp on right left to a pinch, sloper then follow the arête.

57. Lip Smacker
Sds on pinch then out left and throw to the lip.

58. Seam V0
49 35.381N 114 23.301W

59. Little Hulkamaniac*** V2
49 35.497N 114 23.610W
Arête in centre of boulders face. Start standing.

60. Phantom** V3
Sds on jug and out left to the lip. Bad landing. 20 m from Little Hulkamaniac.

Lip Smacker

Phantom

Little Hulkamaniac

Climbing at Frank Slide. Photo: Lev Pinter.

The location of these routes is uncertain. Ask the locals to show you them.

Days of the Phonix

61. Days of the Phonix*** V5
49 35.518N 114 23.586W
Sds on crimps and up left to
sloping edge and up to the jug.

62. Coleco V2
49 35. 515N 114 23. 587W
Double Arête.

63. open project
49 35. 545N 114 23. 605W

Supposedly by the tracks

Coleco

64. Stairway to Heaven ** V5
Sds deadpoint out left and follow
the arête.

65. Spring Board V2
Sds on sloping edge and throw up
to a jug or the arête out right.

Climbing at Frank Slide. Photo: Lev Pinter.

Stairway to Heaven

BIG ROCK

The Big Rock, located in a field about 10 km west of Okotoks, is a large quartzite glacial erratic. The huge barn-sized rock is broken in two main sections, the East and West Rocks. The climbing includes cutter edges, full hand jugs and textbook slopers. In between holds, the rock tends to be smooth and blank. The cracks are wide, clean-angled and far apart. If you are looking for pure power problems that actually top-out with mantles, and lots of highballs, the Big Rock is your place. The problems range from easy to blatantly futuristic. The seriousness of some routes is related to both height and landing. Top-ropes are difficult to rig. Fixed protection is banned.

While the Big Rock serves as a climbing practice area for us, it also fulfils various other recreational, cultural, spiritual and historic purposes for many other people. Mainly because of the Indian pictographs on the south face, there has been considerable pressure applied to ban climbing on the Big Rock by various interest groups. To counter this the Calgary Mountain Club (CMC) is actively involved in protecting climbers access rights. Allan Derbyshire along with Dave Dornian, Stu Slymon and Maya Swannie endured many long meetings with government officals and stakeholders over the years to formulate a compromise solution to meet the needs of the various user groups.

It is very important that all climbers adhere to the following guidelines when climbing on the Big Rock. If we don't do it voluntarily, legislation banning us from the rock completely will be the next step.

1. Avoid climbing near any of the historical Indian pictographs. These pictographs cover a large area, and result in several routes now being considered out-of-bounds. These pictographs result in the South face of the East rock, and the SW corner of the West rock being classified as out-of-bounds.
2. No Fixed Pro
3. No dry tooling (shouldn't this be obvious to everyone?)
4. No modification of the rock (e.g. chipping holds)
5. The only metal to ever touch the rock should be your cams or nuts being gently placed in cracks for top-roping problems
6. Minimize (or preferably completely abandon) the use of chalk. There is a strong possibility of a total chalk ban. If you are leaving any chalk on the rock, you are using too much for this site.
7. Because of the efforts by the CMC, the climbing community is becoming recognized as the main group responsible for cleaning up the area around the Big Rock. Encourage and build on this reputation by always taking a garbage bag out with you, and removing as much litter from the area as you can.

How to Get There

From Calgary, follow Highway 2 south. About 10 km south of the city take the Okotoks exit onto Highway 2A. Drive through Okotoks and turn right (west) on Highway 7 toward Black Diamond and Turner Valley. The Big Rock is clearly visible from the highway. Park in the parking lot on the north side of the highway.

East Rock – South Face

This face is out-of-bounds because of Indian pictographs. Please do not climb on it.

East Rock – East Face

Mostly classic moderate, mellow lines from the beginnings of Big Rock's climbing history.

1. Still on the face staying left of the arete.
2. Good slab climbing.
3. Interesting climbing through a roof and away from a bad landing.
4. More interesting climbing with a key heelhook through the roof and bulging arete.
5. Mellow slab climbing.
6. Mellow slab.

7. Gaining the slabs with a harder move at the beginning and then breaking right and over a roof. It's not as bad as it looks.
8. From the top of the broken blocks climb left of the chimney with a tricky move over the roof.
9. Starting on the boulder gain the large side-pulls and huge jug on the arete then up and left to good hold over the first roof and then out left over the final roof to another positive hold.

10. Mon Cal*** V11
   A long outstanding project that was finally sent in 2001. A heel hook variation drops the grade down substantially. Another sequence uses a big jug half-way out on the roof.

East Rock – East End of the North Face

This is business as far as problems go. High and mentally demanding stuff.

1. **Demaio's Problem**
   This is a prominent and proud highball arete with a horrific landing. Top roped by Demaio and it's not known if it's ever seen a ropeless ascent.
2. **Double Clutch**
   Start in a slight corner and head up to a large double undercling. Then up left to a large ledge and crack to finish. This problem has been toproped since the 70's.
3. Not much is known about the centre of the face. It apparently has been top roped in the 70's and it's not known if it's been highballed.
4. Highball with many variations to start including a jump-start from a boulder on the ground to the prominent lip of the ledge. Either finish direct on desperate exposed edges or traverse left to the obvious fat ledge and then to the lip. From the ledge, the left-most exit is the best option.

West End of North Face

This face is loaded with eliminate problems and contains some of the hardest problems at Big Rock. Allan Derbyshire who has climbed at Big Rock for over 30 years calls it "The Boulderers Face".

1. Sds and follow good holds to flake and finish up corner.
2. **The Flake Route**
   The flake was broken off years ago and is now much more difficult tension problem.
3. **The Resurrection V8**
   Classic hard problem and was the hardest at Big Rock for sometime.
   Starting on the crimps then up to the sidepull and up.
4. **The Re-resurrection V9**
   Starting as for #2 then traverse across crimps and finish as for Resurrection.
5. **The Insurrection V9**
   The sds holds are now broken making this problem harder. Gain the undercling of Resurrection and finish as for that problem.

6. **Jabba*** V12**

   An old Conover project finally sent by Mason with some 35 attempts over a single day. Starting on a sloping ledge with a right hand to a gaston edge and then left to a thin pinch. Left again to a hidden gaston and then set your feet for the huge dyno.

7. **Tauntaun's Trek V11**

   Starting as far left of the face as possible on a right hand undercling and left hand sloper. Traverse right on decent hold to the white chalky pinch block. From there dyno to the big hold to the left of the Resurrection crimps. Traverse across the "Res crimps." Traverse about three more feet and finish up from here.

8. **Wampa's Revenge 7B+**

   Sds on jug then right hand to gaston, left to good ledge, match, left to gaston, right way up to sidepull, pull to the top and use a small break on the flat of the top to top-out. Scary and difficult finish.

9. **Jugs a go-go aka "Firth jug haul"**

   Classic problem climbing from either a sit start or standing on jugs and good edges across jugs and flakes to a desperate slippery top out. Traversing either right or left avoids the complicated direct finish.

10. **Dislocated Traverse**

    Another Jack Firth and Jeff Horne problem that starts as for problem #9 but traverses across jugs high across the face and finishing around #1. Jack once fell of this problem dislocating his elbow

11. **Firth's Corner**

    Another of Jack's problems from the 70's. Layback with the right and big holds with your left. Awkward climbing has made this problem not very popular.

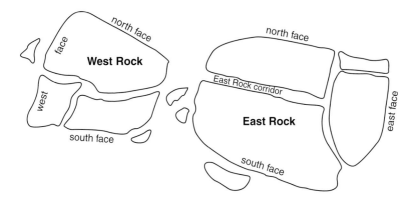

West Corner of the North Face

14. A classic, surprisingly hard and scary bad landing problem.

15. Vulger Up

Starting on the flake and heading up and past the corner. Better landing than #10.

East Rock Corridor – North Wall

1. Climb on the corner just outside of the corridor on good edges but with a bad rocky landing.
2. A Jack Firth and Jeff Horne original that now has a broken-off hold but is still climbable. From the top of this problem you can traverse the lip like the British in the 70's. It is considered to be quite good.
3. Another of Jack and Jeff's climbing up and into the slight layback corner.
4. Easier climbing up the blackened wall on descent edges and then heading out left.

East Rock Corridor – West Wall

Brain Wallace and Bill Stark found three good problems in the 70's.

5. Climb up the black wall and mantle the large block to gain the lip.
6. Good climbing on positive edges.
7. More good climbing on a steep wall with large jugs.

West Rock – South Face

There are pictographs under problem #1 so be sure to keep your feet and fingers far away from this area.

1. Start with both hands above the triangle roof. A hard move with a key heelhook helps to overcome the difficulties.
2. **The Dog Leg Crack**
   Wild bridging moves to a good finish to the crack out right.
3. Standing from the top of the boulder follow the arete to the finish cracks of #2
4. Start with both hands above the roof and then make difficult moves out left then to a good pocket just below the middle of the face. Finish as for #2
5. Start in the middle of the face, move out left to a corner and then out right to edges. Break left across the face and into cracks to finish.
6. Starting on the slabby face head up and right under a slight roof looking for a key pocket and up to horizontal edges and following the flake to the finish.
7. Start to the right of #6 in a slight corner. Head out left across the slabby face under the roof and then from where the roof gets pointed, climb out above the roof on desperate holds to a direct finish on good edges and horizontal cracks. Alternate finish is to the right into the flake of #6.
8. Starting as for #11 head out left to gain the huge bucket ledge of #9 heading out left to the centre of the face (three possible finishes from here) use the undercling with the left and make the desperate move out right to the dish and finish directly up from here.

9. **Undertow** V3/4**

   Sds with hands above the lip to good edge with your right and then a pinch with your left and up right to the huge jug/ledge finishing out left as for #8 and take your pick of exits.

10. **Lip service** V8**

   Starting as for #9 traverse the lip into and finishing as for #11.

11. **Angelina aka "Angel Crack"*** V0+**

   Classic crack problem from the beginning of the British era.

West Rock – West Face

An awesome, imposing and classic face with some desperate problems.

1. **The Brians' Thin V5/6**

   Thin holds with huge gaps between them. This Brian Wallace project sent by Brian Balazs is now considered a classic hard problem.

2. Face climbing to slab finish.

3 & 4. Classic slab routes mostly used as descents off West Rock.

5. Classic chimney.

6. To the right of the Chimney is an older problem from the 70's with a tricky part in the middle. It is recommended that you first top-rope it then attempt a headpoint.

7. **Greenwood Special**

   One of Brians original lines and considered one of the best lines at Big Rock. Three possible starts and two finishes. All variations are all quality lines.

8. Another of the original lines. A fairly direct line climbing the smooth face to some pockets and over a slight roof to a key flake. Then into desperate climbing which is far into the no-fall zone.

9. One of Urs Kallen's toprope routes from the 70's that starts as for #9 and from the pockets traverse right and finish up the prow.

10. **Traverse**

    Start as for #9. When you reach the pockets begin a traverse around the corner and into "The Dog Leg Crack". Continue across the south face in the horizontal crack in the middle of the face. Finish as for #5 or #6 on the south face under the huge triangle roof.

West Rock – North Face

1. A traverse starts from the end of the North face. Stay high on the boulder with your hands just above a horizontal crack and your feet below it. Finishing up a prominent crack.
2. Another original and classic line that finishes as for #1.
3. **Bob's Liquor Mart V9**
   A powerful problem climbed without using your feet. Starting on chest high edges. Hike your foot up to shoulder level and heel or toe hook depending on your height. Then with the left hand to a three finger digit edge and bump with the left to a very thin but, incut edge. Take out the hook and work your feet to position body for a deadpoint to decent edge.
4. **X- Wing V8**
   The single hand dyno. Get into the jug and huck for the next jug and top out.
5. **Y- Wing V9**
   Double hand dyno.
6. **Urs Kallen's Route**
   Another original line from the 70's, strenuous with good side-pulls and a bad landing. Allan Derbyshire calls this Urs Kallen's little party piece.

7. **The American Sandbag Route**
   The British CMC members in the 70s thought it was fun to send visiting
   American climbers up this climb as the top-out on this problem is almost
   impossible and very desperate. Interesting moves off the ground lead to edges
   and a little toss to a diagonal jug with the left. After this jug, the climbing is
   featureless, desperate and hard to reverse.

8. **The Torment of Evil V9/10**
   Starting on the chest high edges of Bob's and traversing across and heading
   for a long reach to a sharks tooth looking edge.

9. **The Full Torment of Evil V11**
   A long problem starting at the left end of the wall as for #1 and traversing
   across, but staying low on edges and jugs (follow the prominent seam) with
   no or little feet and continue as for #8 and then finish by topping out on #6
   by the long reach to the shark fin edge. This problem has been reversed as
   well from the start of problem #7 at an easier grade.

John Lauchlan bouldering at the Big Rock in the 70s. Photo: Urs Kallen

The Erratics Train is a large collection of quartzite boulders that stretches through the foothills of Alberta and Montana. The largest and best know erratic is Big Rock. Weighing in at around 18,000 tons it's a monster and a huge roadside tourist attraction. The second largest is the Glenwood erratic estimated to weigh 2,600 tons. In 1956 *The Erratics Train, Foothills of Alberta* by Arche Stalker was published as a geological survey of Canada report. The report gives descriptions and locations of over 300 boulders from Edson to Glenwood. John Martin used the report to locate and climb some of the more popular boulders in this section in 77/78. Some of these erratics have been blasted away by farmers, others are on private land. The erratics described within this guide provide the best climbing of the documented erratics in the foothills.

The Beddington Area

The Beddington Area contains three boulders and makes a good circuit. The easiest way to climb the three boulders is to start with Split Rock which is now located within the Calgary City limits.

Split Rock by Glenn Reisenhoffer.

Drive north on Centre Street, take a right on Beddington Boulevard, go left on Beddington Trail, then right on Harvest Hills Boulevard. Immediately turning to the right into a golf driving range. The boulder is located about 200 m down the paved trail, down and to the right in West Nose Creek Park. You can see the boulder as you drive over the bridge.

Almost all problems are sit down starts and with the exception of some traverses all problems top-out. Treat this place with respect. It was a spiritual meeting place for first nations folks. Please help clean up any litter.

Photo: Glen Reisenhoffer.

North Boulder

1. **Myles' Mania**
   Sds the north face. Don't sneak off and onto the slab, go for the top.
2. **Master's Edge*****
   Sds. Stay as close as possible to the true NE Arete. You'll feel like Ron Fawcett. Watch out for the little brown bat crack. A classic old problem.
3. **Fang****
   Sds up the east face on some crimpy sharp quartzite.
4. **Easy**
   Sds up the SE Arete. A great warm up.
5. **Fast Eddy***
   Sds up SW Arete. This is the beefier version of Jaime. Start with both hands on the only hold on the arête. Huck for the top of the arête and swing back left onto slab when you can.
6. **Jaime****
   Sds to SW Arete using all the features.
7. **Lao Tzu***
   Sds up west face. No arêtes or sides of rock are used.
8. **Mantel Madness***
   Standing start to a pure mantel onto the west face slab of north boulder.
9. **Neil's Route****
   Sds up NW arête, onto and up slab. A good standing start warm up.

North & East Face

Southeast Face.

10. Marc's Ridge.

Needs a sit down start. Grope the NW Arete as your feet traverse the north face of the boulder and top-out on Myles' Mania.

11. Black Rain*

A sds low traverse from the SE Arete (problem 4) traversing right to Neil's Route. Using any holds below the overlap traverse with difficulty around the Master's Edge (look for the little brown bat crack) and then continue with any hold below chest level to the NW arete.

12. Light Rain

Traverse whole rock using the slab and any hold.

13. Mind Meld***

Sds starting at the NW arête (problem 9, Neil's Route). This problem uses and starts on the sloping holds that form the slab. Grope, grovel and heel hook your way to and around the corner (problem 6). Staying low continue with difficulty in between the rocks and finish on the problem Black Rain. Eat your wheaties before trying this one and of course you can't touch the south boulder when traversing in between the two rocks.

West Face.

South Boulder

14. SE Arete***

Sds climbs the beautifully rounded arête.

15. Crimpy**

Sds up the middle of the east face (not using any arête holds). Watch your tendons as you're crimping. One of the harder problems at Split Rock.

16. Fetus Freddy**

Sds up the NE arête and up onto the east face.

17. Military Larry*

Sds to a problem that starts in between the rocks close to Fetus Freddy. Layaways and edges to the top. The arête is out and so is the wall behind you. An old problem.

18. Three For One

Another in between the rocks problem. If you come off on this one you'll definitely hit the other rock and the holds are small at the top. Sds near the west side of the rock. The problem exists between the NW arête and the second, and more major, left facing ramp of rock. Aim for the tiny notch. The arête and major ramp are out.

19. Gaia.

With a standing start grab any holds along the NW arête and head up with your feet on the north wall. Aim for the tiny notch.

20. Old Age Never Comes
Start standing at the NW Arete and crank up into the dished slab on the west face. A sds would be very difficult.

21. Raw
start standing at the NW Arete (problem 20) and instead of climbing up, traverse and heel hook right until you reach the SW arête and ascend this.

22. Project for someone fit. Someone needs to ascend the west face of the south rock using neither arêtes.

23. Simon Parboosingh Power Hour***
Certainly the hardest problem at Split Rock. This problem ascends the west face with a sds between the south boulder and the MAD Traverse Boulder. Right hand starting on the SW arête and your left where ever you can and huck up the arête with your right hand eventually aiming for a small dish on the lip at the top of the west face. Watch the spine breaking rock behind you.

Note: The routes at Split Rock are not graded. Grade them what you will.

South Rock.

The next four great problems all start at the SW Arete.

24. Slap Me Silly***
Sds with a huck up and slightly right of the arete. Traverse left and grab the fin near the top. Continue left and up. A small dish (same dish as on route 23) at the lip helps execute the final move.

25. Mr. Kinnee***
Sds. When Slap Me Silly goes left you go right and once you can properly stand on the large foothold on the south face head straight up.

26. Side Pull City**
Start standing (some folks use the MAD Traverse boulder to start) and head up and right using only side pulls. This problem traverse the whole south face as it gently ascends. The crux is close to the very end. Top-out on the SE Arete (problem 14).

27. Mr. Kinnee Does Side Pull City***
Sds to the above problem.

28. Little Feet
Sds the left side of the south face. Head for the thin edge where the plate of rock has been broken away. Use the side pulls near the top.

29. Sunday Morning After Church***

Start standing with your right hand on a rounded hold just to the left off the SE Arete (most likely above your head). Left hand on one of the two small edges above your head. This problem has virtually no footholds. Toss up and grab the right sloping large edge at the top of the wall. Try to stick on the wall and head up and over. A very old route (even before sticky rubber). Can a sds be done?

30. Talking to Americans

Sds on The SE Arete and with difficulty traverse into and top-out on Sunday Morning After Church.

31. Fe Fi Fo Fum***

This is a traverse of the south rock starting and ending at the NW arête (problem 20). Start standing and ascend Raw. Sneak around the SW Arete and onto Side Pull City and continue around the rock back to the NW arête.

Mad Traverse Boulder

32. The Mad Traverse**

Sds at the west side of the small boulder that you can easily sit on. Heel hook you're way around the entire boulder until you either burn out or are not small enough to continue. Great fun at the end of your bouldering session.

Crater Rock aka Buffalo Rock

From Split Rock head north on Harvest Hills Boulevard. Then left (west) on Country Hills Boulevard then first right on Country Hills Drive. You are now at the corner of Panorama Hills Way and Panorama Hills Road and Crater Rock.

Train Track Rock
or The Ghetto Boulder
by Glenn Reisenhoffer.

Crater Rock.

Located just outside Coventry Hills. From Crater Rock head east on Country Hills Boulavard. The boulder is pointed, and visible from the road as you cross the train tracks in the distance to the north. Access the boulder via an unmarked dirt road to the north. A good indicator is a large "Harvest Hills Golf Course" sign that is directly across from the dirt road. Please bring a garbage bag as broken glass and litter is a problem.

1. Slippery Slope - Sds.
2. Scooter - Hard up centre of face. Everything is in.
3. Crack Route - Sds.
4. Spray Paint Pricks - To left of Scooter. Standing start.

Daren Tremaine on Unnamed problem at White Buddha.

The Buddha seems to be located in a different climactic region than the rest of southern Alberta. This means bouldering in a T-shirt in January. Most folks seemed to think that this is a flat out lie, but the number of Buddha converts is rapidly growing.

The rock at The Buddha is the sunny southerly outcropping of the same rock formation that makes for good sport climbing at Prairie Creek. Like Prairie, the rock isn't always pretty, but the holds tend to be big and positive, and moves are usually really fun. Gym climbers will feel right at home. The angle of the cliff ranges from 80 degree slab to near horizontal roof climbing. Being limestone The Buddha also has all your favourite holds: pockets, crimpers, slopers, and pinches. Some holds are comfortable and, well... some are not. As for the Buddha—look at the cliff across the valley and see what you think.

Location

The Buddha is located high up on the north side of the Powderface Creek drainage. Park in the Powderface Creek trail head parking lot. In the winter you will find that the gate on Highway 66 (just past the Elbow Falls turn-off) is closed from Dec 1 to May 15. If the gate is closed, park where you can and walk to the trailhead (an invigorating 5 minutes).

Follow the Powderface Creek trail out of the parking lot. The trail begins climbing rightaway in a series ramps and then drops down into the valley and crosses the creek. Once across the creek the trail begins to climb again. As you continue up the trail, look for a small cliff band that angles down towards the main trail on the right hand side. Just past the cliff band, a faint trial on the right heads directly up the slope. Follow this trail as it switchbacks up to the cliff. If you reach a gate on the main trail, you've gone too far.

When to Go

The Buddha faces almost directly south, high on a hillside with very little shade. This means the rock bakes in the sun almost all day. The very best days seem to be the clear, calm early spring and late fall days when the temperature is between 0 and 10°C. October to November and February to March have the most consistent good bouldering weather, but a few good days can usually be had in December and January. Due to the reflected heat you'll often be climbing in a T-shirt and the cool dry air of winter means you'll be able to stick to everything. Being located in the foothills, the weather is often nicer at the Buddha than in Canmore. Beware of Chinooks conditions that promise exceptionally warm weather. The air temp will be very nice but the wind at the base of the cliff has been known to blow away small children. Due to its sunny location, the cliff will start to seep earlier in the spring than most other walls. Unless you've just returned from Thailand, you'll find bouldering in the summer—even in the evening when the temperature drops but the humidity rises—will at least double the grade of most problems.

The Problems

The first thing to get straight about the Buddha is that there are no boulders. Bouldering is done on a short steep cliff, and none of the problems top out. Somebody once told me they had just returned from Fontainbleau and were quite disappointed with the Buddha. Well, don't try to fool yourself; the Buddha is not world class.

Plan view of The White Buddha

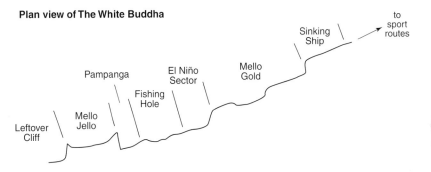

However, two things make the area well worth visiting. The first reason is the weather: it's the warmest cliff in the area. The second reason is that the rock is made for climbing on; the problems here are just plain fun.

The cliff at The Buddha is generally quite short and steep at the bottom. Most problems end at a row of big jugs that conveniently runs across the cliff about 12 feet off the ground. In most places the upper part of the cliff is not worth climbing on. Sit down starts are the rule here and almost all problems are started with both cheeks firmly planted in the dirt.

In a few places the cliff is high enough for some short sport routes. These vary in quality. A few are quite good and you can't really argue with rock climbing around Calgary in February. There are also a few top rope anchors in the Fishing Hole for working out the highballs.

Mello Jello

This is the first wall that you come to as you walk up the trail. You'll know you're there when you see somebody going for a TR burn: sporting a harness, fully racked up with Figure 8, ATC, 2 daisy chains, a full rack of SLCD's, and 6 locking carabiners. Mostly ignored by boulderers, this wall is now the site of some bolted route development.

Poopy Diaper V2
Well it looks like this problem is doomed to fade out into obscurity as it has been bolted and called a route. Just to put a smile on the first ascentionist's face, try the route "winter start" with a sit down start.

Low Traverse V4
The full traverse of this wall extends from the easy scrambling corner to the left of the routes, to the no-hands rest slab to the right. The traverse is broken by a no-hands rest near the sport route "Shake and Bake". The first half of the traverse is easier, sharp, and best avoided. The second half gets the grade and is quite good.

Leftover Cliff

The leftover cliff to the right of Mello Jello.

A. Mountaineers Route 5.2
Who could say no to soloing this ugly, loose corner?

B. V3
Starting on jugs, dead-point up and left to a small edge. Some fancy footwork gets you to the next set of holds and some good rock. Finish in the big pod.

C. V5
Starting on jugs, chuck up and right. Finish in the big pod.

Pampanga

The angle of this wall probably explains why these problems don't get a lot of traffic but they are all very good. The handholds all look big enough that many a first timer has booted up for a nice little warm-up, but the dire lack of footholds usually brings these plans to a quick conclusion.

A   Cross Dresser   V7

This problem traverses the base of the wall from left to right. Start this one standing up with your hands in the pockets just to the right of the corner. The finish is the buckets on the arête.

B   V2

A good intro problem. Starting sitting down, climb the sidepull flakes up and left, finish just right of the start of Cross Dresser.

C   Tri-Star   V5

Start on the jug close to the ground (about 6 feet left of the arête). Fire up to the small pocket, work your way into the undercling, plant your feet and toss for the flat jug at the top of the big black streak. There is a line of bolts continuing up from the finishing hold, but so far nobody has been able to do the route.

D   South-West Ridge   V1

If you don't believe the comment about Pampanga having bad footholds try this apparent jug haul up the arête, with a sit down start of course. Named so that anyone who feels guilty about bouldering in a T-shirt in January—instead of freezing on the one pitch of ice you walked 3.5 hours to get to—can throw out some alpine sounding route names when hanging out with your friends.

E The Rusty Lopez V3

Pockets, edges, and some big pulls on a near vertical wall make it a classic! This problem is on the wall to the right of South-West Ridge. Start sitting down with your left hand in a pocket. Follow a couple of perfect pockets up to some crimpers and the crux. The finish is the two somewhat breast-shaped jugs just left of the corner.

F Leftism V4

Judging by who ferreted out this problem it's not surprising that good crimp strength and a big wingspan make things much easier. The problem traverses from right to left on the same wall as Rusty Lopez. Start standing up with both hands in the big pod and finish on the jugs of the South-West Ridge.

Cross Dresser and Leftism can be linked up and of course, done in either direction.

The Fishing Hole

This is one of the finest walls at The Buddha and home to many of the best problems.

The three bolts and super-shuts on this cliff are there so you can set-up a TR with a few different directionals. If you look in the woods, you'll find a few sticks long enough to put your rope straight into the super-shuts.

A   Two Screwed V1

Start this problem sitting down at the far left end of the Fishing Hole. Follow first the pockets, and then good edges up and to the right along the lip of the ledge. There's a big pod at the right end of the ledge that marks the finish but you kind of have to dig around a bit. Stop whenever you feel you have enough rat piss on your hands.

B   No Show V2

This problem has a brilliant start, but kind of peters out, then finishes on the same dream holds as No Show, ensuring that it will never reach classic status. Start sitting down on a very good but hard-to-find undercling. Climb straight up the big holds in the groove until they fade out, then move a little left on to lower quality rock and the finish of No Show. A much better finish is to start across If Brad had a Hammer then finish on Thach Bich.

C   If Brad had a Hammer... V6

This problem takes on a very steep part of the cliff and makes it feel even steeper by traversing the lip of the roof at a spot where there's almost no foot holds. Think body tension. Start on Two Screwed, then reach way right to the full hand pocket on Thach Bich. Climb to the lip of the roof and then traverse right to finish on the top of the Left Potato Bonda.

At one time Thach Bich was a proud line with a huge pull at the top. But a little loose rock, some careful cleaning ... ah yes, if Brad had a hammer. The good part? There's now two problems that are way more fun than Thach Bich ever was.

D   Hammer Deluxe V8

The full value, deluxe version of If Brad Had a Hammer. Start at the beginning of No Show, traverse through If Brad Had a Hammer, then finish your tour of the Fishing Hole by swinging from jug to jug to the top of Talking Shit. Bring a couple of crash pads and a nimble spotter. One day someone will stretch out Hammer Deluxe right to the top of Q-Tip.

E   Thach Bich V5

This problem is like swinging from rung to rung on your old monkey bars, with a sequence so obvious, you won't even need the little red X's to find the holds. Start sitting down with your hands on a good pocket and an edge. If the first move doesn't drop you on your butt then its just left right left right to the top.

F   Don't Trust Whitey V9
I always thought that this was the blank spot in-between Thach Bich and Left
Potato, but fortunately somebody with enough vision came along to point out
that yet another independent line was lurking in the Fishing Hole. Start
sitting down basically at the start of Left Potato, but with your left hand in
the three-finger pocket on Thach Bich. A big pull to a pinch sets you up for a
couple of brilliant little tacks that require a full range of body funk to stick.
Once you get setup, grab the hand-repelling jug at the lip of the Left Potato
and finishing buckets.

G   The Left Potato Bonda V5
A true classic. It lets you go home with that warm self-assured feeling of "if
that jug at the lip is big, why do I keep missing it?" The starting holds are a
couple of edges just down and left of the black pod, under the first lip of the
overhang. Climb into the pod, get yourself established on the square-cut edge
just over the first lip, then toss. Finish in the big pod above.

H   The Right Potato Bonda V10
An obvious, hard, top-quality line that was scoped early, but went a long
time with out an ascent. So you find a cliff; make a trail; clear out the
landings; clean all the holds; and then some guy shows up one day, sends a
problem and thinks that he gets to name it? (ah, the power of the guide book
author.) Start sitting down on Left Potato. At the square cut edge fire up and
right to the tight little three finger pocket. Finish at the top of Trout Fishing.

I   Staring Into the Sun V11
Same as Right Potato, but instead of climbing
in from the left, come straight out the bulge to
the square cut edge on the first lip. This

variation balances out the problem quite nicely by adding a big right arm pull to the left arm pull on Right Potato.

J   Beatnik V7
Three hard moves that make a more direct start to Trout Fishing. The rats have built a new condo unit right where the problem starts, which makes things a bit more awkward.

K   Trout Fishing in America V6
This was the first problem done in the Fishing Hole and may well be the best at the cliff. A perfect introduction to the harder bouldering at the Buddha. The problem is a big rising traverse from right to left. Start on a juggy edge just down and right of a chest-high, white alcove full of slopers. Fire up into the alcove, then use a couple of pockets to move up and left onto some bad edges. If you can keep your feet on the wall, the finishing bucket is straight above you.

L   Heizenberg's Uncertainty Principle V9
A full right to left tour of the Fishing Hole. Start sitting down on Trout Fishing and start heading straight left under the bulge. (Unfortunately the rock under the bulge tends to be a bit gravely, wet, and crumbly. Plan on doing this bit once a year as the holds should change regularly.) Continue up Left Potato, then across the lip on Brad. Finally top-out up and left of Thach Bich. To keep a sting in it's tail (and the grade) avoid the finishing bucket on Thach Bich.

M   Michi V8
Start sitting down on Trout Fishing. Climb up and left into the edge and pocket complex in the groove. Continue straight up the groove to the rugby ball-sized pod. Not always kind to short people.

N   Dodge This V10
Start on Trout Fishing, Climb straight up the cliff to the finish of Michi. The only catch is that it's an eliminate. The edge and pocket complex (including the sinker three finger) on Trout Fishing are out. If your looking for harder problems this is a nice clean line with lots of fingery face climbing.

O   Talking Shit about a Pretty Sunset V7
The full funk experience. This top quality problem starts in the two "eyes" just right of Trout Fishing and moves up and right on a series of holds that just shouldn't be holds. Pimping like a champion will get you to a good side-pull, and set you up for the finishing toss to the puking bucket with the three foot black tracer, a jug of jugs.

P   Sun-Up V8
For extra value do Talking Shit to the puking bucket, then continue up and right to the super shuts on Q-tip. The traverse moves are great. To date, this has only been done on a top rope.

Q   Brother Number One V8
This problem-which offers loads of powerful, technical climbing-seems to be largely ignored. Starting at the base of Taking Shit, traverse into Q-Tip and head for the anchors. Done on top rope.

R Depth Hoar V7
Three moves of death. This boulder problem is basically the sit down start to
Q-Tip. Set-up on the little crimps just right of the arête and start slapping
until your swinging around on the big pocket at the start of Q-Tip. Theoreti-
cally this problem goes all the way to the anchors but just getting to the
pocket is usually enough.

S Q-Tip V5
This barely-past-vertical face climb is another top rope problem. It features
great moves on some small holds. Set a rope up on the right hand set of super
shuts. Start standing up in the big pocket at head height right where the rope
hangs. Move up and left on a series of edges to a slappy finish. If you're
pimpin' up the slab to the right, you're not on Q-Tip. This problem may one
day get a rope free ascent but the bad landing, and lack of a straightforward
decent, will keep it entertaining.

T Indian Arms Race V3
Start just right of Q-tip hop your belly onto the slab and start humping! A
true sit down has been added which involves trying to palm the very flat
undercling and ups the grade.

The El Nino Sector

Just uphill from the Fishing Hole is the large bulging gray buttress of the El Nino
Sector. This is a good place to get started. The rock here is top quality with holds that
tend to be full hand edges and slopers. However, the landings are a bit funky.

A Doin' Jobz 4 tha Mob V2
A great problem on good rock that feels fairly long. This problem climbs the
corner to the left of the bulge that forms the El Nino Sector. Start with your
hands on the waist-high jugs, with your feet pasted on the wall below. Finish
on the big orange-stained jug just over the lip of roof at the top of the corner.

B El Nino V3
A couple of hard pulls on steep rock. Start sitting down at the left end of the
roof with your right hand on a slopey dish type hold, and your left in a
bizarre, and hard to find little pocket. Finish on Pinned and Mounted.

C Pinned and Mounted V1
Probably the best problem of the grade at the cliff. Moves that flow like butter
over a classic limestone bulge. Start on the left end of a large sloping ramp
that angles down from right to left. Your butt will be very close to a tailbone
shattering rock. Climb straight out the bulge on big edges. At the lip move up
and left to a pod, then a perfect full hand pocket, and the finishing edge.

D   Cadaver Yellow   V3
A little twist on Pinned and Mounted that requires some fancy toe tapping. At the lip on Pinned and Mounted, make a big move straight right to a hold just around the arête. Continue up the arête to a pocket just below the roof.

E   Boot to the Head   V4
A crimp fest up some very steep rock. This problem named itself when a boulderer, going for the second ascent was kneed in the head by his spotter. Despite seeing stars he held on for the assent. The spotter claims it was all an accident, but I'm sure it was jealousy.

   Start around the arête from Pinned and Mounted-way back in the corner under a low roof. If you look around a bit you'll find a good undercling. From here, move up and left on a series of crimper matches until you reach the arête and can finish on Cadaver Yellow.

F   Rat Man   V2
Apparently under the influence of some substance that inspires a utopian view of the world, somebody went looking for a quality problem in the back of the deep v-groove corner, to the right of Boot to the Head.

Mellow Gold Sector

The left side of the Mellow Gold Sector features some of the Buddha's steepest problems. This area is also your best option for colder, windy days. It's fairly well sheltered by its cave-like shape and a natural dirt berm. Some sections of the cliff here are just plain choss; but, there's definitely some classic outings.

The wall that the boulder problem Mellow Gold traverses across is home to an endless series of variations that end on the nice little line of three big jugs about ten feet up. Lots of options for some easier problems and good warm-ups.

A   Work the Jizz V2
It seams that almost every session at the Buddha is started out with a warm-up burn on Work the Jizz. It's the super classic! Start in the back of the corner directly below a yellowish rail that goes straight out the roof. A couple of good laybacks gets you up to the rail-which is an incut bucket. Monkey swing out the rail to the lip of the roof, where you'll find a huge finishing bucket hidden just over the lip.

B   Malcolmhoffer Arête V5
Starting in the corner, climb up the left side of the arête.

C   Hasselhoff Arête V9
The harder version of Segundo. From the sloping gray ledges at the start of
Segundo, move up and left to the tips undercling in the roof. Buckle down
and toss to the arête, then work up to the finish of Segundo.

D   Segundo V8
One of the must-do problems at the cliff. Initially sent using a much harder
sequence, this ascent was concluded with the boulderer discovering just how
slopey the rail to the left of the finishing jug is. Swinging sideways out of
control, and well out of reach of his spotters, he landed with his right foot on
a level patch of grass about two shoe sizes bigger than his foot. Surrounding
the patch of grass were two ankle shredding boulders. Oblivious to what had
just happened he walked away smiling and unscathed while his spotters
examined the landing in shocked disbelief.

    This problem is at the left end of the big roof and is identified by a
beautiful two-pocket at the lip of the roof. Back from the pocket, and a little
to the left are some slopey gray ledges. This is where the problem starts.
Climb straight out and over the bulge, finishing on the blocky edge to the
right of the infamous slopey rail. Anyone claiming the first sit-down start to
this problem will be doomed to a life of ridicule, and the problem of trying to
figure out how to clean the rat shit off their hands.

E & E' 95% Man V9
A good test of your body tension and another must-do problem. Start on
Segundo, when you get the two-pocket at the lip, reach right to the big jug
and begin a mind-expanding, rising traverse of the lip. Finish at the top of
Aruanda on the big rounded yellow jug. Climb a little higher and folks call it
100% Man (C').

F   Beef Cake 4000 V9
Yet another variation on this section of cliff. From the big jug on 95% Man,
move straight up onto the face, then traverse right to the finish at the top of
Aruanda. One day somebody will become my hero by pulling straight up
onto the face.

G   Devolution V5-8
This problem is as hard as you make it. Start in the full-hand pod, to the left
of Aruanda-located in a section of rock that's 'unfortunate' in quality. For the
most sustained outing, stay left and finish on 95% Man. The easier version is
to deke right as soon as possible onto Aruanda.

J Aruanda V3

I'm not sure if anyone has ever bothered to figure out the easiest sequence on this problem, but almost everybody has a favourite variation. Start sitting down with your hands in the big two-handed pocket. Climb up and left on a series of questionable rails to a lip encounter that will require a little more creativity. Finish on the big, rounded, yellow jug.

I Say What You Mean V5

This problem starts at the same place as Aruanda. Instead of moving left on the questionable rails, go straight up the corner on a series of improbable sidepulls. Finish on the big jug on the right side of the corner that comes into reach once you get your feet established over the roof. It's a steaming corner—but don't bother looking for the no hands rest.

H Mellow Gold V4

As long as a route, this problem traverses uphill across some of the Buddha's best rock. Sit yourself down at the start of Aruanda and get busy. The crux is near the start, but the rest is just hard enough to keep you interested. Keep traversing until you've had enough, but be sure to go until at least the second corner. This problem can also be started at the beginning of Segundo, which adds more steep pocket climbing-but also some suspect rock.

The Sinking Ship

Just uphill from the finish of Mellow Gold is a fairly innocent looking gray buttress of bulletproof rock. The problems here are not to be missed. They are very different from the rest of the cliff, and tend to be technical and harder than they look.

A Introduction V0
A good problem to get started on. Climb straight up the left side of the Sinking Ship, on a wall with a gentle angle, and good holds.

B Dave's problem V3
A textbook sloper problem. Things start innocently enough, but you'll soon find your feet have disappeared under a bulge, your hands are pawing a useless sloper and the finishing jug seems a mile away.

C House Wrecker V6
Everything a boulder problem should be. No easy moves, bad handholds, bad footholds, and capped off with a finishing toss to a jug. Start sitting down just left of the deep V corner with your left hand on a good side pull. Finish on the final jug of Dave's Problem. For added value, skip the first big pocket out left, and go straight up the face.

D The Master Plan V2
Climb the deep V-groove corner from a sit down start. Go as high as you feel bold.

Years ago some geological force caused some of the larger bits of choss on Mount Yamnuska to free themselves, and tumble down the scree slope to the valley floor. For years climbers have walked past these blank looking boulders on their way to the easier climbs on the wall above. Now in the new millennium, thanks to plastic holds and large crash pads, local standards have finally advanced to the point where these boulder problems are finally getting done.

As the name implies the rock here is less than inspirational. It is a small area with limited potential. The boulders have mostly been named to keep the crowds away. Who wants to go to 8a.nu and post an FA on the Fairy Boulder?

Location

The boulders described here are the ones that rolled all the way to base of the hill. There are also some very obvious boulders part way up the hill. These have been investigated, but are not covered in this guide. The main attraction up-slope seems to be some very tall near vertical faces. A little effort may turn up some quality lines.

The Big Choss boulder field is visible from the Trans-Canada Highway just after the turn-off to Rafter Six when driving out from Calgary. Park in the Yamnuska parking lot accessed from the 1A highway. You can't see the boulders from the parking lot, in fact they are not visible until you actually get to them. This makes the boulders a little hard to find so you'll have to blindly trust the directions below. From the parking lot follow the gravel road west to a quarry. The road makes a big sweeping right hand turn around the quarry. Follow the road around the sweeping bend, when it starts to straighten out look to the left for a smaller dirt road cutting back in the opposite direction. (Alternatively, halfway around the bend climb up the little slope to your left, then walk through the trees to the dirt road.) Follow the dirt road west until it ends. A faint trail continues from the end of the road and travels straight to the Fairy Boulder. The approach to the first boulder takes about 20 min.

When to Go

Big Choss is located on a sunny south-facing hill but is not as hot as the White Buddha. Summer days are possible but look for cloud and the shady sides of the boulders. Mid September until the first big snowfall is prime with dry rock and crisp weather. Winter is hit and miss. The snow will melt a bit on the south sides of the boulders, but many areas are quite sheltered and the sun disappears behind the ridge at about 3:30 pm. Walking through the main boulder field with a foot of fresh snow can be little hard on your ankles. Spring gets good once the snow melts, but a few of the boulders seep. Snow can also be the great equalizer. A little drifted snow over top of a bad landing can make a flat white tabletop on which to place your crash pad. If you feel like a good samaritan you can run out and sweep off the boulders after each snowfall. Then when the next Chinook rolls through the boulders will be crisp and dry.

A little caution may be required in the fall as hunting season brings a bunch of folks with bows and arrows. They run around in the woods hauling bloody deer carcasses on little sleds.

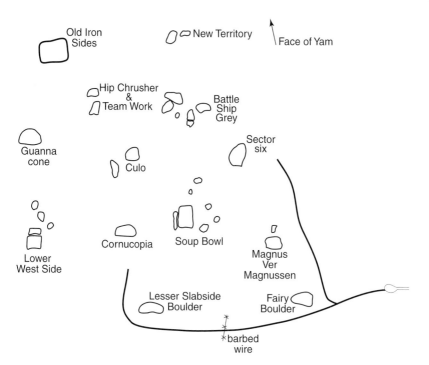

Old Iron Sides

New Territory

Face of Yam

Hip Chrusher & Team Work

Battle Ship Grey

Guanna cone

Culo

Sector six

Lower West Side

Cornucopia

Soup Bowl

Magnus Ver Magnussen

Lesser Slabside Boulder

Fairy Boulder

*barbed wire

The Problems

The rock at Big Choss is old enough that some nice water features are starting to form in the rock. The slide is older than the Frank slide. There are more trees and the rock is more weathered. This means rock with a lot more climbable features. All of the boulders here are limestone. Considering how fractured the rock is, it's a bit scary to think about how big these boulders must have been when they started rolling down the hill.

The holds are mostly edges and slopers, and all of them have very good texture ... maybe too good, as in bloody flapper good. The problems tend to be technical rather than powerful as the boulders are not super steep. Leave your blown out slippers at home. If you have the inclination, a lot of the boulders at Big Choss have very good slab problems.

All of the problems that showed signs of having been climbed before have been left unnamed. If any one cares to claim an FA and or knows the name for these (or just wants to lie) let me know and I'll up date the next edition of the guide. In addition,

Shelly Nairn on The Central Culo. Photo Ryan Creary.

a bunch of the other problems that have been done here are also unnamed. Sometimes it just seems like too much effort to come up with a bunch of names. If you've got some name your dying to use, let me know, and perhaps it could be added. Anything evil or scary sounding will be categorically rejected.

Note: all topos are drawn as top views (except Fairy Boulder) with the main face of Yam towards the top of the page.

Fairy Boulder

The big south face of this boulder rises like a sharks fin out of the grass at its' base. When you first see it as you walk through the forest you'll start to forgive God for giving us so much limestone, but so little that is worth climbing on. The routes, which aren't quite as good as they look, range from just past vertical to all out slab.

A   V0

Lots of different options here to get started. Pick some holds, top out, down climb, invent a circuit...

B   V3

Start on the block in the corner, set-up and toss. Definitely worth doing. A sit start is possible, although harder (V4) it kind of sucks.

C   Zumba   V10

Starting on the far right side of the boulder traverse up and left to the block on the problem above, continue up and left into the crack and top out. This line looks like the lightning bolt symbol for every body's favorite crash pad manufacturer.

D   V6/7

Start up the Directissima then cut out right to the vertical crack on Zumba. Word is it's worth taking a quick look at the top out before going for a burn. Rolling over the top on the FA involved some skin loss as falling off seemed a poor option.

E   V2

The Directissima straight to the top. Just relax... and don't fall.

F   V2

You'll want to be ready for this one. It's not hard, but it's high and well... chossy.

G   V0

You get a good feeling for how high this slab is when you look down and realize that your crash pad looks like a postage stamp, and has slide down the little bank away from the base of the boulder. Everyone has to do this problem at least once. There is also lots of variations from V0 to V2.

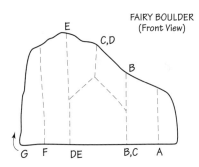

FAIRY BOULDER
(Front View)

The Lesser Slabside Boulder

This boulder, set by itself in the forest, feels like its own little world. The south face is the Webster's definition of a limestone bulge (at least for one or two problems). Finding the boulder for the first time is not straightforward. The best bet is to follow the game trail that heads west from the Fairy Boulder, passing over an old barbed wire fence. The rest of the boulder field is just up hill from here. Once you get the game trail dialled this is probably the easiest way to get to most of the other boulders. A couple of years from now folks will probably get lost looking for the faint game trail, as it will be a well-worn trail.

A   V0
Completely straightforward, but definitely worth doing. A tree seems to have fallen down across the boulder. An ascent may require a saw.

B   Sleeper Wall V0-V1
This short innocent looking wall is not completely that. There are lots of options for problems here with the two grooves being the most obvious. Despite appearances you may have to try.

C   Super Modern World of Beauty V2
Left to right angling crack. Good holds to a more interesting finish.

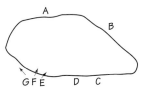

LESSER SLABSIDE BOULDER

Marcus Norman on Full Fly Tai, V7/8. Photo: Daren Tremaine.

D Ol' Pranger V3
You can pretty much start this problem lying down on your back with you left hand on the big side pull. Pull up and grab the edge in the corner with your right hand and continue to the top.

E Shaolin Buddha Finger V8/9
The limestone bulge of your dreams. The thuggish start softens you up a bit for the seeing eye dead point to the Buddha finger. A variety of bad dishes present themselves for the crux, which is hauling your carcass onto the slab.

F Full Fly Tai   V7/8
Haul up to the jug type complex and toss up and left. The edge is crisp but a bit hard to see. Stop trying the move when you start bleeding. Top-out straight up.

G Slag Heap Warrior   V6
This problem is like doing Fly Tai but grabbing a lot of small holds to avoid one big move. From the complex, traverse straight left until it is possible to climb straight up to the edge you toss to on F. If you traverse all the way to the dirty corner then you are on a different problem, and a lot of choss.

Sector Six

This big split boulder is on the east side of the boulder field just as it fades into the trees. Most folks will gravitate to the east side, which is the steepest and one of the coldest places at big choss. If you feel so inclined, the slabs on the south face can get quite engaging.

A Hen Night V2
Start at the far right end of the wall. Traverse left along the rail, climb the corner, and roll onto the slab.

B Blackie Bustos V5
The crack and arête bear hug. Slap from side pull to side pull, and then to the top.

C Mittens McLean V5
Take on the crack directly. A good crisp butt dyno is required to get off the ground.

D Speak Easy V3
This problem starts up the groove on the left side of the perfectly planar section of the wall. Start sitting down with your hands on some combination of blocky edges. Climb up the groove until you can traverse right and top-out.

E Hey Sailor V?
Full value. This problem promises to be one of the hardest at Big Choss. The stand-up start has been done (V6), and all of the moves for the sit start, but full linkage is still waiting to happen.

F V0-2
This face has lots of options for good old fashioned highball slabin'.

G V0
Climb the crack/groove. Easy, and worth doing.

H V0
More easier options, and the decent.

I V0
Just up the hill. A perfect square boulder with nice square holds.

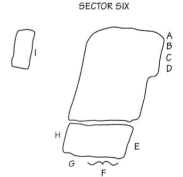

SECTOR SIX

Culo Boulder, Big Iron and The White Fleece

The Culo boulder has some of the nicest water features at Big Choss, as well as some of the sharpest rock. The name was an accident, a bit of a mix-up between couloir and culo. However, once we realized that if we stick with culo the problems name themselves, it was a done deal. For added convenience while warming-up, the problems generally get harder as you work from left to right.

Culo Boulder

A Culo Ridge V0
The worst problem on the boulder, but if your going to do all the problems from left to right then this is were you start. Kind of half sit down grab some edges, and then climb to the top.

B Introductory Culo V0
Find massive jug, climb to top. Dead easy but good. Climbs up past large rock scar.

C Love me Love my Culo V0
Just right of the rock scar. Climb up perfect holds to an immaculate top out.

D Welcome to the Culo V2
Climb the groove just left of the arête. The hardest part is trying to stay in the groove instead of just moving left onto the better holds.

E Me and my Culo V2
The groove on the right side of the arête. Unlike the problem above, this line is great. Start just down and left of the groove. Work your way up and right slowly screwing yourself into the groove until you can grab the monstrous bucket on the lip.

F The Central Culo V3
Straight up the groove in the middle of the face. A sit start and a series of edges leads to a nice little horn type thing just before you roll over the top. Super good.

G Culo Traverse V4
Start on the Central Culo. Traverse up and right to the arête. The ear part way through the traverse is so cool it's worth grabbing a few times even while standing on the ground.

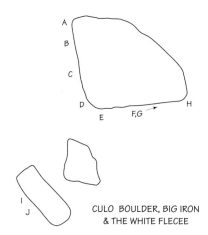

CULO BOULDER, BIG IRON
& THE WHITE FLECEE

Top: Thersa Tremaine on Love me Love my Culo, p. 73. Photo: Daren Tremaine
Bottom: Shaolin Buddha Finger V8/9, p. 71. Photo: Daren Tremaine

H   **Culo Arête V2**
    Grab the big slopey edges just to the right of the arête, paste your right foot
    and dangle your left. Start humping the arête until you can move a bit right
    and pad up the slab.

Big Iron & The White Fleece
  I & J   V0-2
    This boulder has two problems, perhaps even three. They come as a special
    two for one package deal. To claim an ascent of one you really have to do
    both. The rock is flecked with little bits of what appears to be rust.

Guano Cone Area

The Guano Cone is a big boulder with bad landings. This is not the boulder you would want to get
on for a casual little solo session. But then again,
everyone has their own idea of fun.

A   **Left Guana Cone V4**
    Climb straight up the arête. It does get
    easier the higher you go.
B   **Right Guanna Cone   V4**
    Climb up the middle of the face. The lip
    encounter is more interesting if you follow
    the pure line straight up, instead of
    deaking out right.
C   **The Head Stone   V0**
    This little boulder is up and behind the
    Guano Cone. Bear hug the arêtes to the top.
    Not hard but apparently it is aesthetically
    pleasing.

GUANO CONE

Battle Ship Grey

This area has lots of good easy to moderate problems. A good place to warm-up. The snow melts quickly here, but it can also be very windy.

A   Battle Ship Grey V4
The arête. Good rock, nice movement, a bit high, and a bad landing.

B   V2
The right hand arête. The south side of this boulder is nicely overhanging, and has lots of features. A good place to do eliminates if you are so inclined. Most folks climb to the top of the first bulge, then traverses off to the right. If you plan to head up and left, bring a shovel.

C   V3
Start sitting in the hole and climb straight up the centre of the face on great rock

D   V3
Climb the corner at the left side of the face. So far the big block at the top seems to be holding.

E   V0
The simple slab.

F   V0
Left arête.

G   V0
A first-rate problem. Climb up the middle of the face.

H   V1
The righthand arête is also good entertainment.

I   V0
Another slabby adventure. Mind the loose rock.

J   Fru Fru Knick Knack V4
This butt dragger starts sitting down at the left end of the blank roof. Slap and heel hook your way up and right until you can toss up to an undercling pinch, and pull over the lip. Top out if you feel the urge.

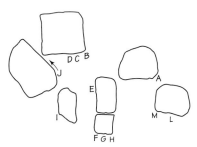

BATTLE SHIP GREY

K   Disco Sit V6/7
All alone on a small boulder, this problem is basically one move. Start sitting down, chuck for the lip. It's just that easy.

L   The pedestrian V0
Very easy but very good.

M   V2
With a little cleaning this could be a good problem.

The Soup Bowl

This area is well worth a visit. It's fairly well sheltered from the wind, but is also quite shady, so pick your days. In the winter, when the sun is low on the horizon, the snow tends to stick around for a while.

A **V1**
Start sitting down. Grab some painful bad rock and thrutch your way to the top. It's all bad.

B **V3**
Start at the bottom of the central groove and make a big move left. Screw your feet around until you can grab the jug and top out.

C **V3**
This is a great problem right up the middle of the face. It's classic Big Choss, small holds on a barely over hanging face.

D **Shwe Tama** **V9**
A bit of an eliminate, but top quality. Pathetic little edges and very balancey face climbing. Start sitting down in the hole just around the arête to the right. Traverse low around the arête then straight up the face. Everything in the central groove is off route.

E **Low traverse**
The feisty start to Shwe Tama can be used to add some interest to the central groove or the left hand line. The grades shake out roughly as follows: Left Low V6, Central Low V6.

F **Misty Steamer V7/8**
First rate arête climbing. Start sitting the hole. A couple of big pulls sets you up for all the arête pinchin' sloper slapin' fun you'll need.

G **Fur Pie V5**
Start from the hole with both cheeks planted on the ground climb straight up to a bit of a committing lip move. More than a few people seem to just hang from the jug at the lip for a while, then drop back down to the ground.

H **Horny for Plenty V4**
The horn at the top beckons, but once in it's clutches you may wish that you didn't actually have to top out. Don't get too creative loose rock can be found.

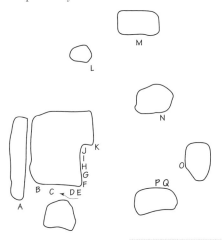

I   Bruiser V4
Yet another problem that starts out of the hole. Go right, then up. Lots of nice big pulls between generous holds. Mind the ones that wiggle especially at the top.

J   V1
Climb the corner, pretend it's fun.

K   V6
Climb the arête from a sit start. It's more than a little deceiving.

L   She Can Do It V0
Lie down on your back and slide under the boulder. Grab the lip and pull over. A fairly safe problem as the crux is knee high off the ground.

M   Things Fall Apart V1
A square face with a big corner/overhang feature. Side pull and under cling the feature to the top. A problem worth doing.

N   Soup Bowl V5
This boulder looks like a wave just starting to curl. Crawl down into the hole at the base. Grab the small edges and climb straight up over the lip. Try not to fall, the landing sucks.

O   V0
Nice face climbing on good rock.

P   V0
Climb straight up the boulder.

Q   V0
The left hand start. If you begin low enough it gets much harder.

Marcus Norman on Shaolin Buddha Finger V8/9 page 71. Photo Marcus Norman collection.

The Lower West Side

There is lots of moderate entertainment here, a few harder problems, and a couple of lines that should become classics. This area is not Big Choss at its best, but it is nice warm sunny place to get started on a cold day. The area basically includes the SW corner of the boulder field. Perhaps one day somebody will wander off into the woods and find another Lesser Slab Side quality boulder, all alone in the forest.

A   V3

Two boulders stacked on top of each other. Sit down, grab the bottom one, climb up onto the top one. I don't think anyone is going to be cancelling any road trips to work on this one.

B   V0

A pleasant trip up a lovely slab. Worth doing for the pistol grip half way up.

C   V2

This is the best of the three lines on this side of the boulder. This problem, which goes up the prow, is nothing but negative down sloping weirdness. Not gym climber friendly.

D   V1

This line has bigger holds and an easier top-out than the problem above, but is not as good. Climb just right of the prow where good rock meets bad. Try to stay on good bits.

E   V3

This problem is much more likely to appeal to the masses. Slightly overhanging, big holds and big pulls. Start sitting down in the hole, climb up and left to the top.

F   V3

Start sitting in the same hole as the problem above, but traverse up and right around the corner, then top out.

G   V0-10

A completely planar face, slightly overhanging, and covered with little golf ball like dimples. It begs to be climbed, but how? The best sequence to date is jump for the top. The grade is determined using a complex formula involving your height, blood type, and the number of crash pads at the base.

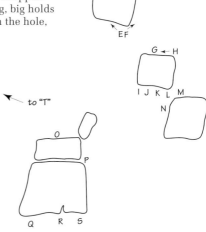

H V2

Still want to climb this face? Haven't quite got the sit-down start figured out? How about a lip traverse? Left to right, right to left, it makes no difference.

I to L V0

Endless moderate entertainment.

M The Flexi Flake V0

Hop on before it's gone. Lie down on your back, grab the flake, and start climbing. If the gods are with you, you won't be the one found lying on your back with a rather large flake on your chest.

N V0

Yet another slab.

O V5/6

A feisty little pimp fest. Start sitting down as low as you can, then crimp your way to the top.

P V1

First rate. Climb the crack and face to the top.

Q V0

Climb the left-to-right angling feature up the face just left of the crack. Go farther left at your own risk.

R V0

Climb the crack.

S V0

Most people will call this a high ball. Climb the face, just left of the arête.

T V1

This problem is all alone straight west of the rest of the boulders in this area. Climb a south facing prow located just right of an Aspen.

Magnus ver Magnussen Area

Magnus is a big proud boulder, with some good hard problems. This area has not yet been well explored. There is still potential for more lines, some will be hard, and a few will be highballs.

A Little Buddy Boulder V0
Somewhere, somebody thinks that this is a good warm-up.

Magnus ver Magnussen
B & C V2
This wall looks very innocent and all, but once you boot up and start heading for the top everything just seems to get bad.

D Atlas Stones V6
The dead obvious line up the left side of the arête. The tendency to barn door into the abyss to the right adds drama to an ascent. This problem awaits a sit start.

E Pillars V5
Start standing up at the arête, make a big iron cross move up and left, then finish on chain pull.

F Chain Pull V4
Climb the face to the mini corner just left of the arête.

The Piss Pyramid

G Left Piss Pyramid V3
This problem starts right above the pointy, sulphur yellow stained rock which has given the boulder its' name. Start with your right hand on a square cut edge, and your left on a triangle just under a roof. Climb straight up to the top.

H Piss Pyramid Traverse V5
Start half sitting just right of the Piss Pyramid with your left hand on the square cut hold and your right pawing nothing but garbage. Climb up and right across some very good rock.

I Right Piss Pyramid V1
This lines has two starts, ones is easier, and one is more fun. Start sitting down on the little ledge at the far right side of the boulder. Great rock.

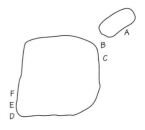

Ryan Johnstone on 69'ers V3. Photo: Daren Tremaine.

Hip Crusher and Team Work Boulder

These boulders are perched up at the top of the slope on the west side of the boulder field. They catch afternoon sun and all of the wind.

Hip Crusher

A   Hip Crusher Traverse V2
Climb up the big right to left ramp to the top. This boulder named its self. During an ill conceived early exploration a boulderer managed to pull off a very large piece of rock near the top of the boulder. The falling boulderer was clearly sailing well over all the crash pads until a selfless spotter body checked him back onto the pads. The end result was one boulderer safely standing on a crash pad and one spotter rolling down the hill. The spotter lost a lot of skin and mangled their hip.

B   Hip Crusher Direct V3
The directissima to the top of the boulder. Start sitting down. Set up on a couple of small edges and perfect little block of a foothold. Pimp straight up the face.

C   Left Hip Crusher V1
Climb the left hand arête to the top.

Team Work Boulder

D   Teamwork Dihedral V2
Climb the sharp, short corner

E   Teamwork Arête V1
Climb the teetering, blocky arête on the downslope face—good but concerning.

F   69'ers V3
A fine example of how a few people and a little determination can turn a bad landing into something suitable for deck chairs and a Hibachi. Start just right of the bulge on a large jug. Move up and left over the bulge to the top.

G   76'ers V3/4
Start in flake, Climb directly up the bulge to the top.

H   33's V2
Left hand arête to face to the left of the bulge.

Old Iron Sides Area

Another area that has currently only seen limited development. If your looking for high balls you've found your area.

Old Iron Sides

A V0
Climb up the far right side of the face on very good rock.

B The Studer Slab V6
If your feeling the magic this is one fine piece of slab. You'll want to put the carbon fibre inserts into your One Sports.

Satellites

C V4
A wave like bulge of very good limestone down in the trees. Try these problems with a few friends. The landing and the lip encounter make things interesting.

D What the Body Remembers V0
Climb up the middle of the boulder.

E V2
A great piece of face climbing. The top-out is just like climbing out of a swimming pool.

F V2
Climb the silver dihedral.

Cornucopia

The low flat boulder, at the top of the hill, as you come up from the Lesser Slab Side. A sunny spot, with easier problems, it's suitable for a casual warm-up.

A V0
A whole world of slabby adventure.

B Shirty V1
Start just right of the arête sitting down.

C V2
Possibly the sharpest and most painful route at Big Choss (which is saying something). Start sitting down below the very bad section of rock. Move up and right along the rail until you can climb straight to the top of the boulder.

D V0
Climb the square prow of rock.

E V0
Climb the face.

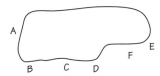

The New Territory

Off in the trees north of the Central Highlands, this area only has a few problems so far, but I'm sure folks will keep running around in the forest, finding new things to climb.

A V3
The righthand sit start. Climb up and left over the bulge. The top-out is quite good.

B V3
The lefthand sit start. Commit to the large block that looks like it will rip off and land on you. Same finish as above.

C V0
The righthand line up the face.

D V1
Climb straight up to the perfect V shaped ridge. A little caution for loose rock may be in order.

Today Rundle Rock is primarily a top roping area, so you might get a few odd looks of disbelief as you attempt a highball problem on the main rock. The highly polished boulders here are all classics as climbers and guides have been visiting the area since 1966. The area is mostly used for learning roped climbing basics.

How to Get There

Approx. 1 km past the Spray River bridge on the Banff Springs Golf Course Road is an unsigned parking lot. Following the map from the parking lot will bring you to the boulders & the main rock.

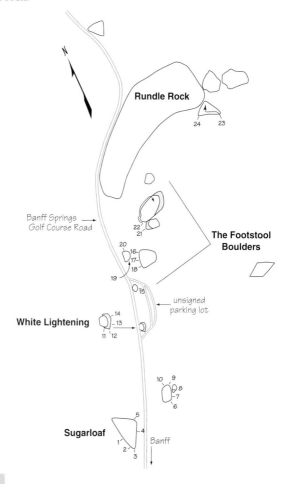

Sugarloaf - aka Mt. Smith

1. Sds on edge & sidepull climbing up & right to big holds. V0
2. Sds on thin edges to edges and back into big holds. V0
3. Climb the slippery arête to top. V0
4. Polished face climbing on edges. (many variations) VB – V0+
5. Climb arête on big edges VB

6. Rising traverse on good edges to top. V0
7. Sds on sidepull to edges & more sidepulls V0+
8. Sds on sm. One handed edge to crimpy face. V1
9. Climb arête directly. VB
10. Low traverse across lip to arête and top. V0+

White Lightening

11. Sds on small crimps to sidepull to sloper & mantle. V-hard
12. Sds on big ledge and up bulgy arête V0-
13. Sds on edges to more edges. (many variations)
14. Sds on flake to big edge & around to arête (many variations) v0

The Footstool Boulders

15. Traverse on edges & lip to trees. V0-
16. Sds on arête to flake & traverse across
17. Boulder on good edges to top. V0+
18. Sds on flake to edges & top V0
19. Sds on undercling to thin face. V1
20. Sds on edges to lip. V0
21. Sds under overhanging arête to crimper & arête slap with a rocking mantle. V5
22. Traverse lip of boulder with technical footwork to top.
    Very bad landing. V4-5

Unnamed boulder by Rundle Rock

23. Sds on arête with rising hand traverse to big jug and top. V0+
24. Sds on edges to thin hold & top. V0+

There is one boulder across from Rundle Rock on the other side of the Bow River that is worth mentioning. Follow the Hoodoo Trail from a trailhead at Buffalo Street. There is a good sized boulder on the left side of the trail near the river. There are two main problems but possibly room for more. Bring a pad as the landings aren't the greatest.

Bow River Boulder

1. Start on chalked hold and v-shaped edge to small crimp/side pull then the heinous sloper. V2
2. Climb arête. V0

Just above the Grassi Lakes sport climbing venue is an excellent bouldering area. The climbing & rock quality is very reminiscent of the Ghetto/Rectory & White Imperialist walls. It will definitely become a popular bouldering area in the future, which will help take pressure off the congested lower canyon on busy weekends.

Warning: This area is still under development so be aware of loose holds and choosy top-outs.

How to Get There
Drive up the Spray Lakes Road from Canmore past the Nordic Centre for 3.1 km to a parking area on the left at Whiteman's Pond. Walk back to the dam road and at the "no parking signs" head up towards EEOR following a faint goat trail for the Lower and Upper areas.

The outcrops are broken into two main areas, lower & upper. The upper area is a concentration of harder unclimbed highball problems, and in one section, compact limestone with some fairly decent landings. Some highball boulders could be equipped with top rope anchors. The lower section has more moderate climbing and is the location of two very aesthetic highballs. The rock and the landings however aren't the best and spotters and pads are required.

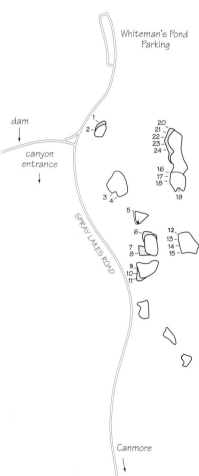

1. **Boulder 101 V0+**
   Sds on big undercling and climb jugs to a mantle top-out.
2. **Boulder 201 V0-**
   Climb big jugs
3. V1+ Left fingers in pocket & right hand on edge climb up two finger edges and scary flake.
4. V1+ Sds in eyes to edges. V0+
5. V0 Traverse boulder on exfoliating rock. Not recommended
6. V? Scary decaying pinnacle
7. V3 Overhanging boulder climbing directly.
8. V3+ Traverse from the left into the overhang.

The Projects
9. The big fin! An amazing but crumbling feature with many variations and good landings. Face climbing on pockets & edges.
10.
11.
12. Rotting limestone
13.
14.
15.
16. The best rock in the areas from pockets to smooth compact sloping limestone.
17.
18.
19.
20.

The Grassi Lakes sport climbing venue has become a popular bouldering area.

How to Get There

Drive up the spray lakes road from Canmore past the Nordic Centre for 3.1 km to a parking area on the left at Whiteman's pond. Walk back to the dam road and descend into the canyon toward the Grassi Lakes for the Swamp Buttress, White Imperialist, Meathooks and Graceland problems. Access to Little China is by walking across the dam and climbing over the fence as for the multi-pitch rock climbs on Ha Ling.

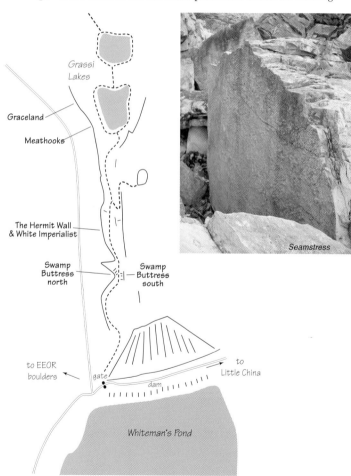

Grassi Lakes

Graceland

Meathooks

The Hermit Wall & White Imperialist

Swamp Buttress north

Swamp Buttress south

Seamstress

to EEOR boulders

gate

to Little China

dam

Whiteman's Pond

Swamp Buttress

North
1. V4 Sds on edges to a sloper and then more edges.
2. Sds and break left to crimps and finish for #1
3. **Sonnie's Problem V6**
4. **Vfun**
   Sds as for #2 and traverse the rail into the sport climb The Deviant.
5. **The Deviant V2**

South
Swamp Buttress North (above and south.

6. **Swamp Left V0+**
7. **Swamp Center V0**
8. **Swamp Right V0+**
9. **Return of the Swamp Thing** ** V?**
   Great looking project, bad landing. Crank the steep edges to sloping top out

The Hermit Wall and White Imperialist

There is an interesting small outcrop above the Hermit Wall still in production. You can approach the problems from the climbers left of the Hermit Wall and follow the drainage (large ice flow in winter) to the top of the cliff.

10. **The Seamstress*** V5**
   Traverse near vertical slab boulder from right to left using just the seam.
11 **Chinatown Cave**
   Get down and dirty in the back of the Chinatown Cave.

Return of the Swamp Thing

Meathooks Area

12. The Legend of Sleepy Hollow*** V?

To the right of Meathooks Wall is a cave with an entrance about 5 feet off the ground. Start in a huge hueco in the back of this cave. Cimb out of the roof on good horizontal jugs, sticking to the left and into a two finger pocket. Finish on a jug on the headwall outside of the cave. Put on a harness and link it up with a the newly bolted sport route above the cave (see Sport Climbs In the Canadian Rockies)

The Legend of Sleepy Hollow

Graceland Area

To the left of the sport climb You Ain't Nothin' but a Hang Dog is a bench in a dug-out.

13. Premarital Sex*** V2

Sds Crank out right and out of the roof to a positive jug and a throw to the lip.

14. Safe Sex V6***

Sds then out left and direct on rail crimps to the left and finish as for #13.

15. Sds and crank to the crimps of #13 and finish.

16. A traverse link-up with the Gracleand routes would be good fun. Not known if ever attempted or completed.

Safe & Premarital Sex.

Chinatown Cave

Little China – Upper Section

This area has received some notorious slander from a couple of internet chat lines. Less Talk More Rock! The problems are still fun even though they're on the shorter side. The area was developed by Dung Nguyen and his junior team.

Fortune Cookie

1. **Soft & Spiky*** V1**
   Surf both arêtes
2. **Skin on Fire*** V2**
   Start on right face, link-up Soft & Spiky
3. **Ne t'arrête pas** V1**
   Traverse left, follow righthand arête.
4. **Katana** V0**
   Start on arête, left to corner
5. **Ninja* V0**
   Face up with right arête
6. **Samourai* V0**
   Face up with left arête
7. **Chow Chow** V0**
   Climb clean face

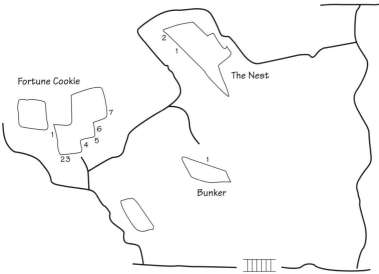

The Nest
1. **Vol au-dessus d'un nid de coucou** V2
   Start from the face, lightly diagonal left up.
2. **Cric, Crac, Croc** V1
   From the crack, move up right.

Bunker
1. **Slicky** V0
   Friction up on obvious face.

Little China – Lower Section

Shelter
1. **The Vision** V6
   Sds under overhang, pull lefthand face.
2. **Midget Power** V5
   Stand up start. Climb up the middle face.
3. **Linoleum** V4
   Stand up start. Crimp up right face.

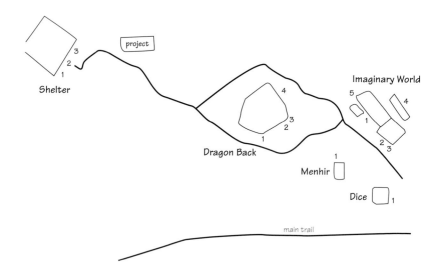

Dragon Back

1. **Orange Peels** V2**
   Traverse left, follow right hand arête
2. **Shoot & Score** V3**
   Surf both arêtes
3. **C'est y piquant*** V3**
4. **Dragon Flair* V1**
Start on arête, left to corner

Menhir

1. **Idefix* V0**
   Kiddy problem

Dice

1. **5' and under** V1**
   Sds crank and mantle.

Imaginary World

1. **Demetane ** V3**
   Straight up the face
2. **Renatane * V0**
   Short face climbing
3. **Hong Kong Fu Fu V3****
   link #1 and #2
4. **Albator *** V4**
   Sds crimp up the overhang
5. **Astro V0**
   Commit to right hand corner, face left.

JURA CREEK

The canyon walls of Jura are perfect for bouldering. Water–worn scoops and long traverses are prevalent in this tight canyon and some harder slippery testpieces are waiting for an ascent. The first recorded bouldering in Jura Creek was in the winter of 2000 by Louis-Julien Roy, Shelly Nairn, Dung Nguyen and Paddy Jerome. Because of the canyon's good aspect, winter bouldering during a decent Chinook winter is recommended as snow covers up a lot of the rocky landings. Climbing in the early spring isn't recommended as the canyon will be a torrent of water. This area is still under development with potential for many more problems, so bring along a sturdy brush and give'er.

How to get There
Located 1 km east of Exshaw on highway 1A. Fifty metres from the guardrail and creekbed is a small pull–out with very limited parking. Walking down the highway to the guardrail and up the creek cobbles brings you to the mouth of the canyon in about 10–15 minutes.

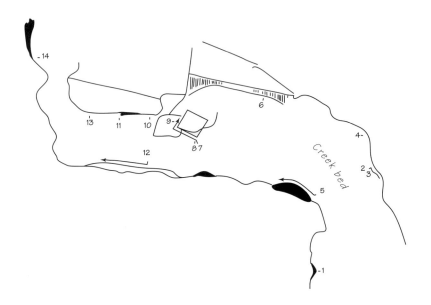

Top: Shelly Nairn on East Side Finger Crack. Bottom: Paddy Jerome on the Sugar Cube. Photos: Louis-Julien Roy.

1. Sds Climb out short roof. V0
2. Sds Climb out short roof. V0
3. project out of polished scoop
4. Top rope overhang
5. Traverse lip on good edges.
6. **East Side Finger Crack V0**

The Sugar Cube

7. Sds and campus to jugs then out right to the arête and the lip V2
8. **Sugar Cube Traverse V2**
9. Face climbing many eliminates V1
10. Climb the arête. V3
11. Crack climb V0
12. project
13. project
14. project

Jura project

Jura # 10, 11 & 13

The Sugar Cube.

Jura # 13

Trailside Boulder at Takakkaw Falls. Photo Ryan Creary.

TAKAKKAW FALLS

Located in Yoho National Park near Field B.C, Takakkaw Falls is the second highest waterfall in Canada and is a major summer tourist attraction.

Getting There

Follow the Yoho Valley Road which leaves the Trans-Canada Highway just east of Field to the parking lot and trailhead for the falls. If you follow the trail to the falls you will come to a good boulder on the right, Trailside boulder. From this point head to the left under rock walls and across a broken boulder field to the main area far from the hideous numbers of tourists. The area has nice climbable sized boulders of featured dolomite limestone with many high quality problems. Some classic problems were sent in the summer and fall of 2001 by the late Chad Lucier, Nick Furfaro and Matthew Hedman. A larger development of the boulders occurred in the fall of 2002, by Dung Nguyen and Chris Fink. Other contributors were Mattieu Ellie and J. F. Giroux.

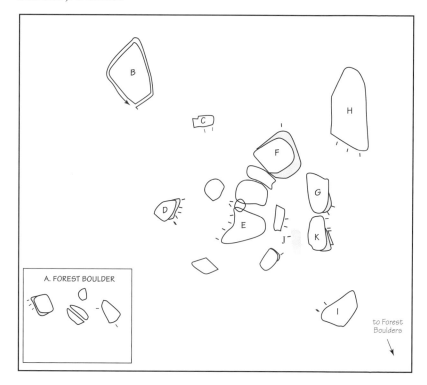

Trailside Boulder

1. **Another Tourist Attraction*** V3**
   Sds Many possible starting holds
   move out right with heel hook up to
   flexing flake. Continue up on good
   holds. Many eliminates exist but the
   grade seems to stay the same.
2. **V0**
3. **V0**

A. Forest Boulders

1. **V1****
   Sds on arête and up to edge and positive jugs
   to finish.
2. **V2*****
   Sds on edges and deadpoint to crimp and then
   edge and another power move to incut hold
   and top out.
3. **V1****
   Sds on edges and move out to right to good jug
   and into the crack to the top out.
4. **V2***
   Sds on arête and up.
5. **VB***
   Face.
6. **VB**
   Sds on edges up to more edges, jug and top out.

B. Girlfriend Boulder

1. **V0-**
   Traverse of entire boulder

Above 2 photos: Trailside Boulder

C. Surfer's Paradise

1. **V0****
   Sds surf the lip on good
   holds.
2. **V?****
   Sds or not climb face to
   pointed top. Project.

Kiddy Boulder

   V0**
   Sds under roof on positive
   holds, short problem.

Surfer's Paradise

D. The White One

1. Triple F. V6***
Sds on the arête with small crimp and sloper and to pinch and then good edge and sloper. Left to edge on face and continue on lip on arête to mantle.

2. White Unicorn V4**
Starting on sidepulls in an iron cross up to tight crimp and awkward sloping sidepull then the lip.

3. V3**
Starting with both hands on a positive crimp move out far right to sidepull and powerful move to a jug and the lip.

4. (project)
Traverse from both-hands crimp as for #3, then across to tight crimp and match edge of problem #1 and the lip.

The White One

Hans Solo Boulder

E. The Han Solo Boulder
1. **Crack VB***
2. **Freakish Friday V0+****
   Steep flake
3. **Project V?****
   Steep face project
4. **Arête VB***
5. **Off-width VB**
6. **Arête VB**

Giant Slab Boulder

F. The Big White One
1. **Nothing Yet**

I. Liquid Boulder
1. Crystal Method V1**
Sds on positive holds and direct to top out.
2. Liquid Lunch V1**
Sds on positive holds and direct on jugs.

J. Giant Slab Boulder VB
Many problems and cracks to choose from.

K. Triangle Face
1. **V0***
   Sds Traverse lip to pointed top.
2. **Project**

J. The Room
1. **Dusty V2****
   Sds on two jugs and up and left on
   flake and good edge to top out.
2. **VB**
   Climb positive edges
3. **Trick or Treat V5*****
   Sds on good holds and blind throw to
   sloping lip. Then up to knob and left
   to positive edges and top.
4. **Trick or Treat Direct V4*****
   Same as #3 then knob and mantle up
   to good edge up and right.

Triangle Face

K. Balls Out Boulder
1. **Balls Out VB*****
   Classic! SS Crack in center of face.
2. **French Kiss V3****
   Sds under Balls Out then break right
   to parallel crack.
3. **Boob Show V4/5*****
   Low traverse on good holds and
   crimper to the Sds holds of #4. Finish
   as for #4.
4. **Smells Like Bishop V1****
   Sds on good holds and power to good
   holds and finish out left or out right
   on face.

Above, right & below: The Room

Lev Pinter climbing at Cathedral. Photo Marcus Norman.

This unique area is nestled at the foot of majestic Cathedral Mountain and its sister peak Cathedral Crags. The bouldering consists of both quartzite and limestone boulders ranging from 2 to 20 meters in height. These rocks follow large slide paths that have cut their way downhill through the forest to the river below the highway. An ecologically sensitive area; one must tread lightly and adopt a "zero-impact" attitude, especially when opening new problems.

History

Word on the street is that this area has been visited as early as 20 years ago. No doubt routes like "Wak Crack" received first ascent a few years ago, but those responsible have kept it quiet. The true name of this mini-route may someday come to light. It is unavoidable that some problems/rocks will receive names that contradict earlier ascents. This is simply due to lack of available information. Modern ascents can be credited to a number of people including Randy Coleman (who has spent a considerable amount of effort in development), Lev Pinter, Scott Milton, Chris Fink, Derick Gallaway, Dung Nguyen, Marcus Norman, Seth Mason, Dave Thompson, Greg Dickie, Rich Castillo among others.

Access

Drive 17 km west of Lake Louise on Hwy #1 to a pull-out called "Spiral Tunnels" where tourists take photos of trains entering the valley below. This is where you park. The closest boulder, creatively named "First Stone", is located slightly upslope across the highway in the trees. You can see it from the parking area.

Season and amenities

This is a summer bouldering area with a weather-dependant season based on snowfall. June through September is probably the best time to go. Cushy Lake Louise is nearby for easy camping, hostelling and hotels. A number of fine restaurants are located in these hotels for the gourmet climber hog. Be sure to check the seasonal camping restrictions at:

http://www.discoveralberta.com/ParksCanada-Banff/trailreport.html

Considerations

Obvious steps must be taken to avoid impact and preserve area access:
1. Don't get run over by cars or trucks
2. Don't cut down live trees or build trails – it is a **Federal Offence**
3. Be gentle with moss beds – clean only the absolute minimum for safe climbing – **this could affect access if neglected**
4. Be wary of wildlife – this includes grizzlies, black bears, wolverines, hoary marmots, wolves, mountain lions and fat ravens. All of these live in the area and can eat you (although it is unlikely)
5. Don't walk on tracks and cross them quickly. Don't mouth off to CP employees if encountered; you do **not** have a right to walk on CP property—**see Malamute, Squamish access issues** for a result of climber vs. CP (you can guess the result)
6. There is a voluntary **bolting ban** for this area

Cathedral Forest

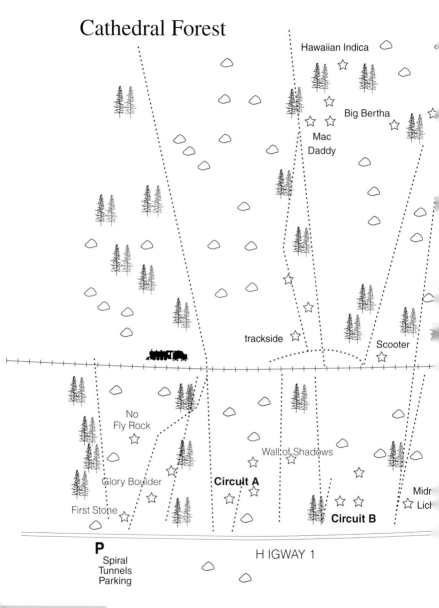

Hawaiian Indica

Big Bertha

Mac
Daddy

trackside

Scooter

No
Fly Rock

Wall of Shadows

Circuit A

Glory Boulder

First Stone

Circuit B

Midr
Lich

P
Spiral
Tunnels
Parking

H IGWAY 1

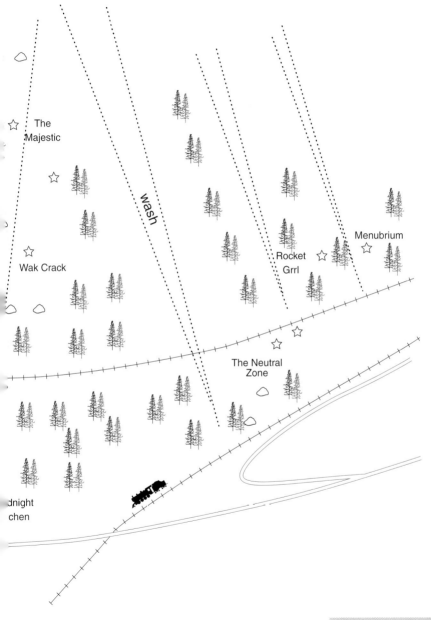

The Majestic

wash

Wak Crack

Rocket Grrl

Menubrium

The Neutral Zone

dnight
chen

First Stone Area

The first area above the parking lot offers fun problems on good quartzite

First Stone

Home to the first problems at Cathedral, many eliminates zig-zag the entire back and side face. From left to right:

1. **Magic Heel* V1**
   Sds far left edge of face, up and right.
2. **Unknown** V1**
   Sds middle of face.
3. **Arbor Arête* V2**
   Sds left of arête, climb up arête.
4. **Reisenshine* V2**
   Sds face right of arête up crimps.

First Stone – back

5. **First Stone Traverse* V5**
   Traverse left on rail through crack around corner to Magic Heel.

The Birdseed

This innocuous little rock has 2 Fontainbleau-style problems on it. Good fun.

1. **Nova** V4**
   Sds slopes up left to top.
2. **Ova** V4**
   Same sds as #1. Up right.

Glory Boulder

Home to a tricky face route "Glorificus", the backside of this rock offers several powerful lines. From left to right:

1. **Double Bonza V1**
   Traverse from left, finish on 2
2. **Quack V4**
   Sds. Bulge through left side of arête.
3. **Fingerf%*#* V6**
   Sds. Crimps to crack to jug.
4. **Lev's Foster Child*** V6**
   Sds. Low sidepulls to start, slap arête, to left dish on top, finish up right.

5. **Glorificus* V3 HB**
   Crimps up face through top.

No Fly Rock
This steep face has one line. A good idea is to brush off the top holds as a fall could hurt.
1. **No Fly Zone V3 HB**
   Face, arête, through top

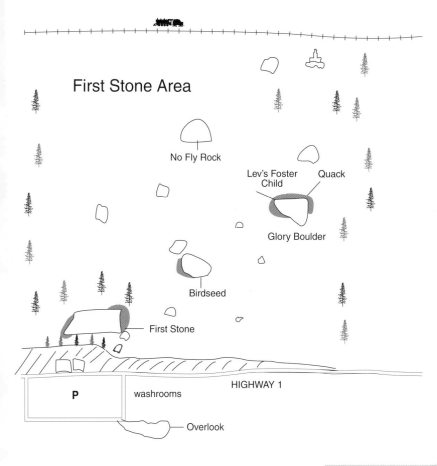

First Stone Area

No Fly Rock

Lev's Foster Child

Quack

Glory Boulder

Birdseed

First Stone

HIGHWAY 1

P

washrooms

Overlook

Circuit A

Wall of Shadows aka The Big Brawl

A great block with several classic lines. Also has the potential for hard vertical eliminates

1. **Little Brawl V0**
   Sds up sidepulls to top.
2. **Beautiful Butterfly*** V2**
   Sds. Edges to sloper to top.
3. **Krakatoa*** V4 HB**
   Sds. Crack to top.
4a. **project**
   Branch left up smooth face
4b. **Other Good Crack** V2 HB**
   Sds up crack to top.

The Big Brawl

Flake Rock

A good bulging arête can be found here. Watch out for the tree!

   Unknown Arête V2**
   Bulging arête, flake is out, to top.
   Arching Flake V0

Tora

   Tora Traverse* V1
   A good warm-up. Sds. Rail from left to apex.

Silverfish

1. **Silverfish Arête* V2/3**
   Sds. Up left side to top.
2. **Silverfish*** V6/7**
   Sds. Edges up steep face to top. Powerful!
3. **Deceiver** V3**
   Sds. Rail up right arête to top.

Mushroom Attack

   Left side V0
   Sds under bulge.
Several other V0s are found to the right for warming up

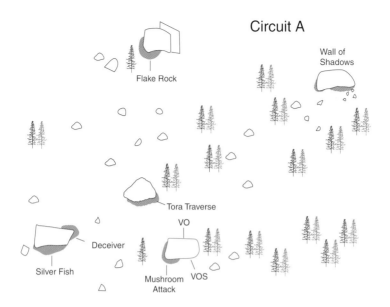

Circuit A

Flake Rock

Wall of Shadows

Tora Traverse

VO

Deceiver

Silver Fish

Mushroom Attack

VOS

Circuit B

Circuit B offers quick access to great quartzite in close concentration. More potential exists in this area to expand.

Midnight Lichen Boulder

A 5-star rock with bomber holds on a steep face

1. **Midnight Lichen*** V4 HB**
   Sds low in crack, up and left on crimps to top.
2. **Scott's Simple Huck** V4**
   Sds as 4, top out to right.
3. **Seams Likely*** V3**
   Sds as 4, follow seam out right, finish up arête.
4. **Hale Bob* V4**
   The back of Midnight Lichen has a deceiving 1-move problem. Sds. Crimps to top.

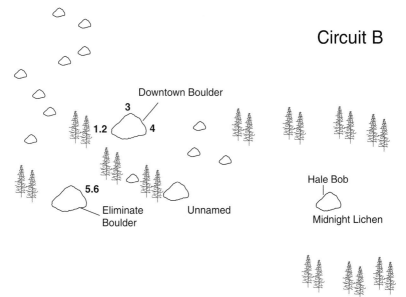

Downtown Boulder

3

1.2 **4**

Hale Bob

5.6

Eliminate
Boulder

Unnamed

Midnight Lichen

Unnamed
Up slab to top V4 HB

Eliminate Boulder
An excellent steep bulge with great holds
5. **Unknown* V2**
   Up face to top.
6. **Unknown*** V4/5**
   Sds low and right, up slopers to top.

Downtown Boulder
An interesting quartzite block with several tricky traverses
1. **Unnamed** V4**
   Sds. Face to top.
2. **Way Down** V8**
   Sds. Traverse from #1 around arête into #3.
3. **Downtown** V6**
   Sds. Follow seam from right to left, up dirty face to top.
4. **Unknown V2**
   Sds. Crimps to jug.

The Neutral Zone, Defiant, Rocket Grrl Areas

One could spend a whole day on these testpieces

The Neutral Zone

An imposing and powerful cliff. Full top-outs are possible although not mandatory. All problems start deep in the trench. Left to right.

1. **Fully Functional*** V5**
   Sds start deep in trench with ass on low rock. Follow flake up and left to either high left jug or top with care.
2. **Killer Robot Crack** V6**
   Sds as per #1, bust up crack to finish on sharp pocket/jug above right.
3. **6 of 9*** V9/10**
   Sds up hourglass feature to top rail.
4. **Khan** V5**
   Sds on low rail in trench, follow flakes straight up to corner jug.
5. **Malcolm in the Middling* V4**
   Sds as pre #4, traverse right on highest rail.
6. **Go Left* V4**
   Sds as #4, traverse right on lower rail.

Defiant

A powerful piece of marble, harder and better than it looks. Left to right.

1. **Janeway* V4**
   Sds, undercling, up through crimps, slopers, break left into break.
2. **Defiant*** V6**
   Sds as #8, straight up slopers.
3. **Borg Me** V8**
   Sds just right of #8, up and right to finish on top-out of #11
4. **Low Profile** V5**
   Sds as #10, follow steep seam with right hand, left on face, top-out on jugs to right.

The Neutral Zone, Defiant, Rocket Grrl Areas

Rocket Grrl Rock

A huge chunk of limestone, this rock offers several great warm-ups. There are many straight-ups and eliminates on front face.

1. **Rocket Grrl Traverse V2**
   Sds right side, follow rails left.
2. **Groovy V3**
   Sds on jug, edges to below moss, finish right into hole.

Menubrium

1. **Menubrium V9/10**
   Sds. Traverse out left to bad sloping hold.

Trackside Area

This extensive area provides many challenging problems on solid quartzite blocks up to 40 feet in height. A great circuit!

Trackside Boulder – aka Chopper
A 5-star piece of stone with 2 classic problems not to be missed
1. **Dwarf Toss*** V6**
   Center of face to v-shaped hold to top. Not kind to short people (sds has not been completed).
2. **Swordfish Arête*** V5**
   Sds in obvious low jug and low roof undercling, out right on face to arête to apex.
   The Cleaver V4/5**
   Sds. Crimps to lip, exit left.

Unnamed 1
   Sds. Right face V0
   Sds. Left face V0

Unnamed 2
   Sds. right face V2
   Sds. left face V2

Copperhead
1. **Rusty Nail* V3/4**
   Sds. Low traverse right to left.
2. **Rusty Spike V0**
   Sds. High traverse, start as #5.

Trackside Boulder

TNT
Two great problems on this "egg"
   TNT V3**
   Sds on flake, straight up, finish right.
   C4 V3**
   Sds as TNT, traverse right, finish right.

Scooter
A surprising rock offering two fun problems, one that is harder than it appears
1. **Hypa Hypa* V0**
   Sds. Left face.
2. **Scooter** V4**
   Sds in flake, up right to top.

Scooter

Trackside Area

Hawaiian Indica

Dihed

Majestic Rock

Unnamed 3

Mac Daddy

Big Bertha

Thug Tug

TNT

Unnamed 2

V2

V2

Unnamed 1

V0

V0

Copperhead

Wakk Crack

Trackside

Scooter

Wakk Crack Block

Wakk Crack*** V3 HB
Steep hand crack to top.

Unnamed 3
2 great problems with steep starts.
6. Unknown. Cave sds. Finish left.** V2
7. Unknown. Sds. Climb out of cave.** V3

Mac Daddy
A large, imposing rock with a steep west face and north cave. Head up the boulders above Trackside Boulder, keeping to the right edge of the slide. 100 yards (approx.) up, cut into the trees. This huge block is hidden from the boulder field. It can also be accessed via Big Bertha.

Mr. Roper* V6
Start right, smooth face to broken seam.

Cave routes
All projects. An excellent problem was put up here but a key hold fell off making it rather harder than the initial V8

Dihed Block
1. **Travolta* V1**
   Sds low, top-out right.
2. **Sphincter* V6**
   Sds low and right in 2-handed flake, up through crimps left to top.

Big Bertha
Across the slope from Mac Daddy, this big rock has good potential on its north face. Its west face is very steep and tall – the site of a potential testpiece

Dihed Block

1. **Lady of the Wood** V5 - HB**
   A bold FA considering the highest hold on the face looked rather dubious, and the top-out was still dirty. Start in crack/seam. Up high left face to top-out left.
2. **Unnamed* V2**
   Sds right side of boulder, up and left to finish on rail.

Hawaiian Indica Boulder

A large block, its west face is steeply undercut offering one problem. It has potential for several hard eliminates and traverses. The north face is tall with several warm-ups

Rip Curl*** V7/8
Sds low in cave. Right on sidepull, up to sloper to top.

The Majestic Rock
The Majestic*** V5
Sds. Rail in from left, pull bulge to pocket to top.

In the Trees
Just above Thug Tug. This rock offers delicate face climbing on bomber rock. From left to right

1. V2 Slopey face, exit up and left.*
2. V2 Arête to top.
3. V1 Sds. Dihedral to top.**
4. V1 Slab to top.
5. V2 Sds. Short arête.*

Thug Tug
Hidden in the trees, this pretty block surrenders 3 problems. All of good quality.

1. V1 Sds in crack, follow up and left to top.*
2. V2 Sds as per 1, slap next rail, follow to top.**
3. V3 Sds as per 1, slap rail, then right to arête to top.***

In the Trees

Thug Tug

WEEPING BOULDERS

In the sun bleached Saskatchewan Valley the stunning rockwalls of Mount Wilson's Weeping Wall have created horrendous amounts of rockfall over the years, and as a result legendary amounts of bouldering. The Weeping Boulders consist of a high quality, compact limestone, with incredible arêtes, rooms, roof cracks and ancient pocket-filled coral reefs. The number of potential problems and hard projects will keep dedicated boulderers busy for years to come.

Although the area has been explored over the years it is David Marra who first recorded the sport climbs on one of the larger house size boulders. (See The Jasper Rock Guide Book). It's not known who bolted the 2-bolt Corner Crisis climbs that have now seen many ropeless ascents. The Reef also has sport climbs on it's ancient sloping pockets and huecos, but it's not known when they were put up.

How to Get There

The Weeping Boulders are located on Hwy. 93 (Icefield Parkway) about 27 km north of the David Thompson Highway. Park at the Weeping Wall pull-out, and walk back south about 100 m to the boulders.

Season

Climbing is possible year round and makes you question why Canadians migrate south in the winter to climb? With a decent Chinook combined with this already potent sun trap you'll be able to climb here in Feburary. In the spring the boulders are home to wood ticks, so watch out from April until the big dry spell sometime in June. Some of the rooms and caves are often wet, dark and cold in winter and spring and are best left until mid summer.

Accommodation

The Rampart Creek Hostel is comfortable and is somewhat affordable. The Crossing Resort, a pit-stop located near the David Thompson Highway junction, offers accomodation, fuel, a cafeteria and pub. The next closest amenities are in Lake Lousie, some 80 km farther south.

Photo: Ryan Creary.

Chris Fink working on a project at Weeping Wall. Photo Ryan Creary.

The Lauchlan Boulders

This small collection of sharp alpine boulders have potential for some hard futuristic testpieces. Only one of the four boulders (Lauchlan 1) has recorded climbs.

1. **Close Call** ** **V1**
   Sds and climb face on good edges.
2. **Coral Reach** ** **V0**
   Face climbing on good stone and finish as for #3
3. **Paddy's Problem** ** **V0**
   Traverse from #2 onto the flake and up into the large hueco.
4. **Project**
   Sds out of cave on good jug and throw out to the lip and finish up the corner.
5. **Project**
   Low traverse of across entire boulder and finish as for #4.

Laughlan 1

Laughlan 3

Laughlan 2

Laughlan 4

Warmup Wall

The BronX

Project V-Hard
Sds on hueco and throw for sloper
out left, then right to a pinch and
deadpoint to a three finger edge.

The House Boulder
No problems yet. All sport.

Warm Up Wall see photo page 121
Variations in the Vb range.

Corner Crisis Boulders
Short sport routes that can be bouldered
with excellent landings.

1. **V1-V2*** Sport routes.**
2. **Corner** Vb**
3. **Crisis** V2/3**
   Balancey face climbing on small
   crimps and then edges.
4. **Project**
   Stacked roof problem above corner.

Sport Routes

Sport Routes

Corner & Crisis

The Reef

Amazing ancient coral reef with a couple of unknown sport climbs and one absolute classic problem.

1. **The Shark Fin Arête*** V3**
   Sds on arête and climb horizontally to sloper with the left and good pocket with the right. Body tension and scumming are required to gain the wobbly flake lip and edges above.

   The Rat Guano Cave Project
   Horizontal roof hand crack deep down in the mungy cave.

The Reef

Shark Fin Arête

Rat Guano

The 45 Degree Boulder

Amazing pockets and edges on solid stone, lots of future projects.

1. **Flight Attendant*** V6/7**
   Start standing left of the arête on flake and up a two-finger pocket and a viscous dyno for the finishing jugs.

The Stacked Boulders

Projects with nasty landings.

Paddy's Boulder

1. **Unnamed** V0**
   Good climbing using pockets with the right and the crack out left.

2. **Unnamed** V0**
   More good climbing on good rock.

45 Degree

Stacked Boulders

Paddys Boulder

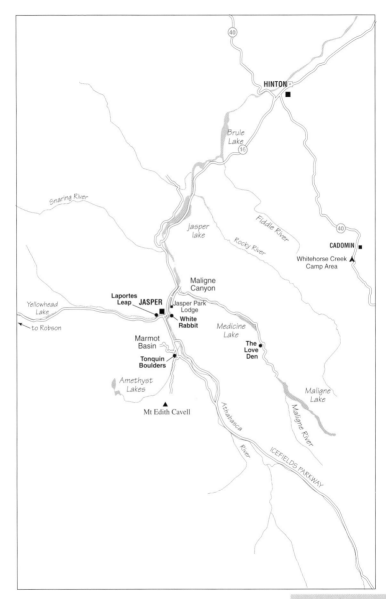

Laporte's Leap

A small outcrop of gritsone and slate just a kilometre west of Jasper on Highway 16. The sunny south-facing slab of slate is Laporte's Front. Laporte's Rear is the shady wall of hard gritstone in the back. Laporte's Leap is another part of our bouldering heritage with some of the oldest problems is the Rockies. A majority of the problems are high and it's recommended that they are toproped, or led with gear.

Laporte's Front

1. **Laporte's Bulge V0**
   Scale the bulge at the far left of Laporte's Front. Might be a little choosy! Not shown

2. **Laporte's Dihedral VB**
   The easy dihedral left of the main slab.

3. **Easy Face VB**
   The Easy Face between the dihedral and Left Crack. Many variations.

4. **Left Crack VB**
   The obvious crack on the left side of the slab. Easy top-out.

5. **Slabmaster V3**
   Just to the right of Right Crack is a thin seam (extra thin fingers). Trent Hoover will personally dub you a slab master if you send this super-thin crack. No running starts.

6. **Right Crack VB**
   The crack on the right.

7. **Flake de Laporte VB**
   The excellent lieback flake to the right of Right Crack.

8. **Three Cracks V1+**
   On the right side of the slab (closest to the road) are three horizontal cracks. Starting just to the right of the lieback flake (Flake de Laporte), climb up through the three cracks. Mind-expanding and scary!

Laporte's Rear

(Open Project) V8? Trent Hoover calls this the perfect problem; high and powerful. Trent also boasts this is Jasper's version of Midnight Lightning and has yet to receive an ascent. So get on it! Start on the low, small, sloping edge, and move up into the seam, then to a small dish at the lip, and mantle up into the huge sloping dish.

Hobo Rock

Located a short distance back behind Laportes Leap is a small bluff of gritstone just past an awkward area of dead fall you'll have to scramble over. This rock has potential for a couple of harder problems with just as hard landings.

Laporte's Rear

Hobo Rock

The Love Den

The Love Den is a collection of limestone boulders several km past the far end of Medicine Lake, in Jasper National Park, Alberta. Although there's only a few developed boulders here, the quality of rock is worth the drive. Solid, with beautiful sweeping bulges and heavily pocketed stone. The Love Den was first discovered and developed in 1993 by three dedicated Edmonton boulderers, Greg Toss, Aaron Pellerin and Dan Archambault.

How to Get There

A short distance east of Jasper Townsite on Hwy. 16 is a turn-off to Maligne Lake and Jasper Park Lodge. Follow signs toward Malign Lake for approximately 32 km. After passing Medicine Lake you will come across a large lefthand bend in the road. About 2 minutes beyond the bend is a small unmarked overgrown pull-out and very limited parking (car pooling from the Jasper townsite is a good idea). A good indicator is to look for several boulders (one close to the road) and many larger boulders up to the left on a hill. The Love Den Boulders are to the right of the road. The pull-out turns into an old access road. Follow this for about 10-12 minutes to the first rock area.

There are two recommendations for boulderers.
1. Stay away from The Pride Rock area as it's a choss pile.
2. Bring at least 3 crash pads for problems on the Cube as the finishing moves are high and cruxes.

First Rock

1. **Fremen** ** **V6/7**
   Start on flat ledge and go straight up. Use a small crimp for your left hand and move to a good right handhold straight up, avoid big foothold to your right, the arête is out. The original version skips the crimp with a dyno at V8.

2. **Unnamed** ** **V2**
   Start on jugs not using the arête, follow the jugs and edges to a big pocket straight up and then top-out.

3. **V4/5**
   Traverse "Fremen" into "Unnamed"

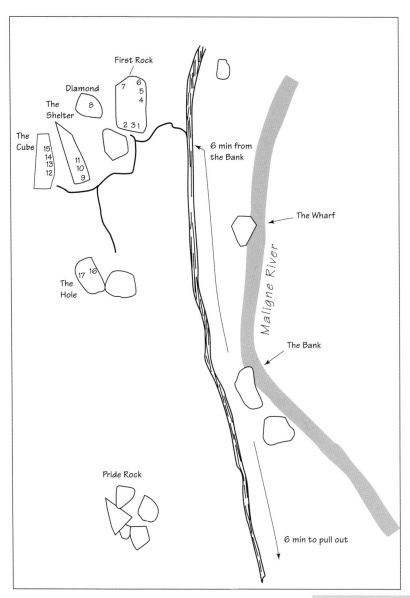

First Rock

Diamond

The Shelter

The Cube

7 6
   5
   4

8

2 3 1

15
14
13
12

11
10
9

6 min from the Bank

The Wharf

Maligne River

The Bank

The Hole

17 16

Pride Rock

6 min to pull out

Seth Mason on Oompaloompa V9 , The Love Den. Photo Ryan Creary.

#7

Diamond in Rough

4. **V0**
   Climb right of arête.
5. **V1**
   Climb left of arête.
6. **V4****
   Climb interesting block pinches direct.
7. **Vb- V3**
   Sunny exposure with variations.

8. **Diamond in the Rough*** V10/11**
   Sds on ledge and then right hand to a pinch on the corner. Huge move out with the left to a crimp and tricky toe hook to a match on the ledge and another toss to a sloper out right.

Shelter Boulder

9. V4/5**

Start on the big hueco, go up staying to the left, small holds to a good hold over the lip, and finish up the arête.

10. V4**

Start as for #9, move right and into the 2/3 finger pocket, left to the small crimp and then throw to good ledge out right and finish directly.

11. Only the Strong* V10

Sds on crimps to a gaston out right and dynamic awkward but precise deadpoint out left to a crimp and the finish.

The Cube

12. Spice Melange** V10
Start on left facing side-pull and traverse right, up to a small crimp with the right a huge throw to the yellow streak with the left.

13. Oompaloompa*** V9
As for #12 but left hand to crimp and right hand to other yellow streak.

14. The Tossinator** V7
Start as for #12 and traverse out right and up to finish.

15. V6**
Start right hand in pocket and left hand side pull and continue and finish as for #14.

The Hole

16. Everybody but Seller*** V3
Climb up out of the hole.

17. Holey Mantle* V5
Start on the opposite of #16, use small edges as gaston to big left power move to top-out.

The Hole

Tonquin Boulders

There are two boulders here: the Tonquin Boulder and the smaller Sureshot Boulder. These limestone boulders have almost no ground cover and have been perfectly excavated by the eroding water of the Astoria River. The boulders top and sides are smoothly water-worn and the boulders bases now have karstic or cave like qualities such as toothy cracks, fissures and slots. These boulders are one of the Jasper Area's hidden jewels and have some serious world-class potential!

How to Get There

From Jasper, drive south on the Icefields Parkway for 7 km. Turn right onto Hwy. 93A and follow it to a bridge over the Astoria River about 2.8 km beyond the Marmot Basin turn-off. Park off to the left at the Edith Cavell Road Trailer Drop-off. Just after the bridge on the left side of the river is a dirt road. Follow this road for about 50 m, then drop down to a trail on the right that will take you to the river and the boulders.

Tonquin Boulder, north face

1. **Ninja Magic** V8**
   Sds, right hand underclinging the positive "insect head" hold, and head up the steep arête on blocky holds to gain the sloping shelf and edges up high for moves up and onto the slab. The climbing is desperate after this point and turns a fun problem into a nightmare and most opt out for down climbing and the safety of the ground.

2. **Geidi-Prime** V9**
   This problem finishes at the jug half way up the west face of the boulder. A highball finish into "Silverfish" still remains to be attempted.

3. **Silverfish V9 (Project) HB**
   Start as for #4 but from the giant side-pull head out left and then straight up the face toward the highest point of the boulder. A direct start is possible at V8 called "Silverfish Direct".

4. **First Time for Everything* V3**
   Sds with your hands in the lowest yellow "toothy" slot. Use the smoother slots to head up and right, first to the nice smooth mini-jug, then the giant gaston/sidepull, then right again to jugs.

Tonquin Boulder, northwest corner

5. IG-88* V11**
   Sds right hand to great gaston edge. Yard up and out left to seam edge. Right
   hand slaps to another twin-edge seam edge. Right hand slaps to another twin
   edge. Work feet and stand up to huge edge and then to the huge layback jug
   and finish as for #4.

6. Felix's Problem V9
   Sds as for "IG-88" and left hand goes to side-pull. Right hand grabs top of the
   seam to your right. Left-hand launches way up to twin seam. Right hand
   comes in as intermediate to work feet then right hand to the finishing jug of
   "Mandalorian".

7. Euphoria (As it Relates to Bouldering)* V5**
   Sds as for #8 and traverse left into the underclinging slot. Left hand slapping
   straight up into the weird 'toothy' crack to gain the sloping rail of
   'Mandalorian' with your right and finish as that problem.

8. Mandalorian V10**
   Sds in huge underclinging seam. Right hand way up to vertical seam into good
   jug. Left to the sloping rail and cross through match and shoot left to weird
   angled edge, right falls into edge by your face. Left to prickly finishing jug.

Tonquin Boulder, west face

9. Sullust V9

S. Mason 2002. Same start as "Mandalorian" Left crosses through to great edge in the seam. Right goes out to obvious undercling edge. Left comes in to undercling edge. Left or Right hand shoots to the twin edges breaking the face. Wrestle over lip and out into the moss.

10. KP* V3

Start on the obvious slot on the middle of the south face of the boulder; head straight up and onto the slab.

Tonquin Boulder, south face

11. Start low on southwest corner, up into slopers, mantle up.

12. V1

Start as per "KP", head right then up to little bush.

13. Up and Down* VB

The easiest line up the middle of the east face. Watch the landing.

Sureshot Boulder

1. **Sureshot* V1+**
   This problem is left of the boulders southern arête. Start with your hands on the rail at mid-height, set your feet, and push for the top. One of the original problems and is now the finishing moves for #2.

2. **Shug Nixx V12/13**
   Project. Sds way at bottom of roof, on good undercling holds. Slap and undercling your way out of the roof for the crux of throwing out and over the lip to good holds and the top out.

3. **Sureshot Traverse V5**
   Start on northwest side. Traverse right along horizontal crack to thin face moves. End standing on support boulder.

4. **Annies Route V3**
   Goofy

Also reported are climbs on Sureshot west face and east face.

The White Rabbit Boulders – Paul Martin & Mick Levin

The White Rabbit Boulders are located near Old Fort Point, a 30-minute walk from Jasper Town Centre and a 15-minute walk from Jasper Park Lodge. The problems are all very short, but offer heaps of fun on slightly overhung rock that features solid edges and pockets. Bring tape for your tips as a lot of the edges are quite sharp. Very little further development exists without extensive cleaning which locals feel is environmentally unacceptable. Routes are graded easy, moderate and hard. It's up to you what numbers you want to put next to them.

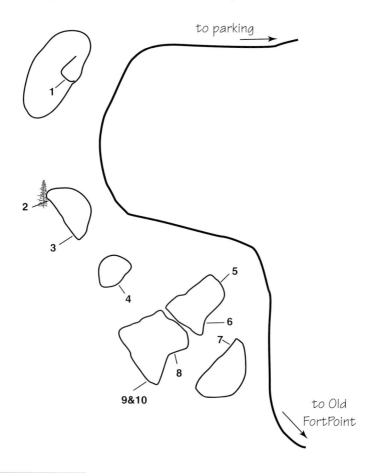

How to Get There

From Jasper follow Highway 93A south. This is the only road heading south across the tracks from the main drag near the centre of Jasper. You can also access the 93A from Highway 16. After crossing (or turning off) Hwy. 16, take the first road to the left, cross the Athabasca River bridge and turn into the Old Fort Point parking lot. From the parking lot follow Trail 1 (**not** the stairs to Old Fort Point) for approximately 3 minutes and the boulders will appear on the righthand side of the track.

1. Unnamed (easy) The crack to righthand traverse was probably climbed ages ago though the wall to the right has some potential for a hard sit-start problem.

2. **Through the Looking Glass** (hard)
    Sds. Traverses the boulder from bottom left to top right. Find the **huge** undercling on the bottom left side of the boulder. Start matched in this. Go to pockets, (no resting on the tree!) head up then right to good hold, right again to slopers and boulder top, match on good flat top and jump off.

3. **The Cheshire Cat** (hard)
    Sds at small edges left of arête, slap up right to a good edge and follow the line through the little rooflets to finish as for #2. Note: an easier sit-start variant (moderate) climbs the arête by starting around to the right.

4. **π**
    Look for the Pi symbol on the rock. Information unavailable.

5. Unnamed (easy) Sds at big jug. One-move wonder to next big jug and step off.

6. Unnamed (easy) Sds at arête and edge. Straight up and top over.

7. Unnamed (easy) Stand-up start. Up right side of arête—looks to have been climbed previously.

8. **White Rabbit (moderate)**
    Sds at twin edges in scoop to left of arête. Move straight up scoop keeping left of arête, gain flat tops at boulder top then move right to arête to top out (around?!).

9. **Alice** (moderate but hard if you're a short-arse)
    Sds at nice hold under hanging arête/bulge. Move out arête/bulge on edges (look for sidepull on right side of arête/bulge to sloper on nose. Move right again to jugs, traverse right to finish as for #8.

10. **Alice RHV** (hard)
    Start as for #9. Traverse under arête/bulge to tiny crimps on its righthand side, up to jugs and finish as for #9.

CADOMIN BOULDERS

Cadomin has a future as being a bouldering mecca of northern Alberta. The potential for new problems and the amount of unclimbed boulders is staggering! You'll have to do a little exploring of the treed slopes and the upper plateau of Luscar Mountain to find these gems, but you'll be amply rewarded with some fine pocketed limestone and some excellent rock quality if you search long enough.

Warning: Some of the boulders have a lot of loose holds and a majority of the tops are extremely loose so, heads up! Don't feel obliged to top out on every problem especially if it's a choosy mantle to finish. Just down climb or drop to the ground and save your skull the fracturing.

How to Get There

Located 50 km southeast on Highway 40 from Hinton is the sleepy village of Cadomin. Approx. 6 km out and past Cadomin is the Whitehorse Creek Recreation Area. This is the campground and the home of some fine established problems.

In Cadomin you'll find Jacoby's Mountain Road General Store & Hole in the Wall Café which offers camping and fishing supplies, gas, propane, post office, telephone, offsales and licensed dining lounge.

Cadomin also has the "Cadomin Caves" to explore and makes an excellent rest day activity. The fishing in the area is also excellent with rainbow trout, brookies, brown trout, cutthrout, and Rocky Mountain whitefish.

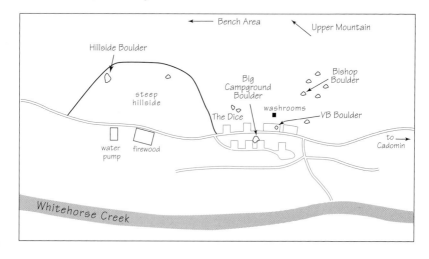

Big Campground Boulder

1. **Mom's V1**
   Sds. Head straight up arête. Move up and right to top out.
2. **Howling V2**
   Start on big pocket and head up and left to big slot.
3. **The Valley of the Wind V9?**
   From the start to the lip it's got roughly 32 moves. Start on the slab on the right side of the boulder in the big pocket, traverse left across the overhanging face, staying relatively low, and finish on the top out of Mom's
4. **Whatever V1**

VB Boulder

5. **Ancient Sea VB**
   Traverse the slab from right to left, finishing up the left-hand arête. Easy moves on clean rock.
6. **Easy Arête VB**
   The obvious arête.
7. **One Hand, One Pocket VB**
   The nearly vertical, pocketed face that faces the washrooms.

Bishop Boulder

8. **Lonely Man V3**

Big Campground

Hillside Boulder

9. **Pocket Protector V? (project)**
   Sds on thin edge and two-finger pocket. Climb out sickly steep roof on thin pockets to the lip and finish.

Pocket protect

Upper Mountain

Bench Area and Upper Mountain

More projects on good rock.

Selected Alpine Climbs in the Canadian Rockies

Sean Dougherty, 320p., $19.95
An up-to-date guide to the best mountaineering routes in the Canadian Rockies.

Sport Climbs in the Canadian Rockies

John Martin & Jon Jones, 336p., $29.95
Sport climbs in the Bow Valley west of Calgary.

Bow Valley Rock

Chris Perry & Joe Josephson, 432p., $29.95
Multi-pitch climbs in the Bow Valley west of Calgary.

Banff Rock

Chris Perry. Due spring 2004.
Rock climbs in the vicinity of Banff.

Ghost Rock

Andy Genereux, 336p., $24.95
Rock climbs in the Ghost and Waiparous areas.

Scrambles in the Canadian Rockies

Alan Kane, 336p., $24.95
A guide to non-technical peaks for mountain scramblers.

Waterfall Ice Climbs in the Canadian Rockies

Joe Josephson, 400p., $29.95
A wide selection of ice climbs on both sides of the Canadian Rockies.

Mixed Climbs in the Canadian Rockies

Sean Isaac, New edition Fall 2003
The latest in mixed climbing routes.

To order, write or email
Heritage House Publishing
#108, 17665-66A Avenue
Surrey, BC V3S 2A7
distribution@heritagehouse.ca
Or visit our web site at **www.rmbooks.com**